15 MINUTE
JAPANESE

15 MINUTE
JAPANESE
LEARN IN JUST 12 WEEKS

MITSUKO MAEDA-NYE
SHIZUYO OKADA

DK

London, New York, Munich, Melbourne,
and Delhi

Senior Editor Angeles Gavira
Project Art Editor Vanessa Marr
DTP Designer John Goldsmid
Production Controller Luca Frassinetti
Publishing Manager Liz Wheeler
Managing Art Editor Philip Ormerod
Publishing Director Jonathan Metcalf
Art Director Bryn Walls

**Language content for Dorling Kindersley by
g-and-w publishing**

**Produced for Dorling Kindersley by
Schermuly Design Co.**

First published in Great Britain in 2005 by
Dorling Kindersley Limited
80 Strand, London WC2R 0RL
Penguin Group (UK)

4 6 8 10 9 7 5
002-196117-May/2013-book
193207-May/2013-pack

Copyright © 2005, 2013 Dorling Kindersley Limited
All rights reserved.

A CIP catalogue record is available for this book
from the British Library
ISBN 978-1-4093-3115-5

15 Minute Japanese is available as a book on its own,
in an audio pack with two CDs, or as part of a
complete language pack.

Printed and bound in China by Leo Paper Products LTD.

Discover more at
www.dk.com

CONTENTS

How to use this book

The main part of this book is devoted to 12 themed chapters, broken down into five 15-minute daily lessons, the last of which is a revision lesson. So, in just 12 weeks you will have completed the course. A concluding reference section contains a menu guide, an English-to-Japanese dictionary, and tables of Japanese characters.

Warm up
Each day starts with a 1-minute warm up that encourages you to recall vocabulary or phrases you have learned previously. The time in brackets indicates the amount of time you are expected to spend on each exercise.

Useful phrases
Selected phrases relevant to the topic help you speak and understand.

Cultural/Conversational tip
These panels provide additional insights into life in Japan and language usage.

Text styles
Japanese script and easy-to-read pronunciation are included, as well as the English translation.

In conversation
Illustrated dialogues reflecting how vocabulary and phrases are used in everyday situations appear throughout the book.

How to use the flap
The book's cover flaps allow you to conceal the Japanese so that you can test whether you have remembered correctly.

Review and repeat
A recap of selected elements of previous lessons helps to reinforce your knowledge.

Instructions
Each exercise is numbered and introduced by instructions that explain what to do. In some cases additional information is given about the language point being covered.

LEISURE AND SOCIALIZING 123

招待者
shohtai sha
hostess

4 Words to remember (3 minutes)
Familiarize yourself with these words and test yourself using the flap.

party	パーティー *pahtih*
invitation	招待 *shohtai*
gift	お土産 *omiyage*

Read it You can now distinguish the three Japanese character sets and recognize some basic recurring words. Use the tables on pp.158-9 to look back over the lessons and see how much more you can read.

Put into practice (2 minutes)
Join in this conversation.

土曜日にパーティーを開く のですが、お暇ですか？
doyoh bi ni pahtih o hiraku no desuga, ohima desuka

We are having a party on Saturday. Are you free?

Say: Yes, how nice!

ああよかった！何時に伺い ましょうか？
ah yokatta! nanji ni ukagai mashohka

That's great!

Say: At what time should we arrive?

とう

atoh gossaimasu inviting us.

ですね！
esune
e!

ご主人もご一緒に。
goshujin mo goissho ni
Please bring your husband.

何時に伺いましょうか？
nanji ni ukagai mashohka
At what time should we arrive?

Say it
In these exercises you are asked to apply what you have learned using different vocabulary.

5 Say it (2 minutes)
Do you have any single rooms?
For two nights.
Is dinner included?

Pronunciation guide

Most Japanese sounds will already be familiar to you, and the pronunciation guide given for all words and phrases in *15-Minute Japanese* is designed to be natural to read. However, a few sounds require additional explanation:

r	a Japanese r is pronounced like a cross between an English r and l
ih	*ee* as in sh<u>ee</u>p
eh	long *eh*, like a longer version of the sound in th<u>ey</u>
oh	long *o* as in m<u>o</u>tor
final u	the final u written on the end of words such as *desu* (is/are) and *(ga/a) arimasu* (there is/are) is only slightly pronounced and often sounds more like a double letter (e.g. *dess*).

The Japanese language is based on syllables, rather than individual letters. Each syllable is pronounced with roughly equal stress.

Read it
These panels help you understand how the Japanese script works, present useful signs, and give tips for deciphering Japanese characters.

ku-koh
airport

Read it Here's another example of two *kanji* characters combining to make a separate meaning:
空 (**ku**, sky) +
港 (**koh**, port).

Dictionary
A mini-dictionary provides ready reference from English to Japanese for 2,500 words.

144 **DICTIONARY**

DICTIONARY
English to Japanese

The plural is normally the same as the singular in Japanese. In general, Japanese descriptive words, or adjectives, may change depending on how they are used. Some of these adjectives are followed by *(na)* or *(no)*. If a noun is used following a particular *kanji* we have put *kanji wo kireh no* *(an)* *(ga/a)* *(a ga/o getY)*

Menu guide
Use this guide as a reference for identifying popular Japanese dishes on the menu.

128 **MENU GUIDE**

MENU GUIDE
This guide lists the most common terms you may encounter on Japanese menus. Dishes are divided into categories and the Japanese script is displayed clearly to help you identify items on a menu.

Starters and soups

hamu	ハム	ham
ohdoburu	オードブル	hors d'oeuvres
otsumami	お つまみ	Japanese appetizer
tsukidashi	つきだし	Japanese appetizer
su shi	寿司付け	lobster
meron	メロン	melon
misutorohbai	ミネストローネ	minestrone
kuruma ebi	車えび	prawns
smohku sahmon	スモークサーモン	smoked salmon
misoshiru	みそ汁	soup made with fermented bean paste
tomato supu	トマトスープ	tomato soup

Egg dishes

behkon eggu	ベーコンエッグ	bacon and eggs
tamago	卵	egg
medama yaki	目玉焼き	fried eggs
hamu eggu	ハムエッグ	ham and eggs
tamago yaki	玉子焼き	Japanese omelette
omuretsu	オムレツ	omelette
omuraisu	オムライス	rolled omelette filled with rice

1 Warm up (1 minute)

The Warm Up panel appears at the beginning of each topic. Use it to reinforce what you have already learned and to prepare yourself for moving ahead with the new subject.

KONNICHIWA
Hello

The Japanese bow is famous: the lower the bow, the more respectful. Traditionally, there would not be any contact in the form of a handshake or kisses. With the increasing Western influence, the Japanese now often shake hands, sometimes bowing at the same time, especially when meeting foreigners.

2 Words to remember (6 minutes)

Say these expressions aloud. Hide the text on the left with the cover flap and try to remember the Japanese for each. Check your answers.

こんにちは。
konnichiwa
Hello!

おはようございます。 *ohayo gozaimasu*	Good morning.
こんばんは。 *konbanwa*	Good evening.
私の名前は...です。 *watashi no namae wa...desu*	My name is...
どうぞ、よろしく。 *dohzo yoroshiku*	Pleased to meet you.
さようなら。 *sayohnara*	Goodbye. (formal)
さよなら。 *sayonara*	Goodbye. (informal)
ではまたあした。 *dewa mata ashita*	See you tomorrow.

3 In conversation: formal (3 minutes)

こんにちは。
私の名前は岡田です。
konnichiwa. watashi no namae wa Okada desu

Hello. My name is Okada.

こんにちは。私の名前はロバート・バーカーです。
konnichiwa. watashi no namae wa Robahto Barker desu

Hello. My name is Robert Barker.

どうぞ、よろしく。
dohzo yoroshiku

Pleased to meet you.

4 Put into practice (2 minutes)

Join in this conversation. Read the Japanese beside the pictures on the left and then follow the instructions to make your reply. Then test yourself by concealing the answers with the cover flap.

こんばんは。 こんばんは。
konbanwa *konbanwa*

Good evening.

Say: Good evening.

私の名前は前田美樹朗です。 どうぞ、よろ
watashi no namae wa しく前田さん。
Maeda Mikiro desu *dohzo yoroshiku Maeda-san*

My name is Maeda Mikiro.

Say: Pleased to meet you, Maeda-san.

Conversational tip The Japanese usually introduce themselves using either just the family name - Okada - or the family name followed by the first name - Maeda Mikiro. But they are used to hearing Western names the other way: Robert Barker. It's not common to ask someone their name directly, so listen carefully to the introductions. When talking to/about others, you should add the honorific *san*, but don't use *san* when talking about yourself. Levels of formality are inbuilt into the Japanese language and it takes time to acquire a feel for this. This programme will introduce you to polite, but not overformal, Japanese.

5 In conversation: informal (3 minutes)

ではまたあした？
dewa mata ashita

See you tomorrow?

はい、ではまたあした。
Hai, dewa mata ashita

Yes, see you tomorrow.

さよなら。
sayonara

Goodbye.

WATASHI NO KAZOKU
My family

1 **Warm up** (1 minute)

Say "hello" and "goodbye" in Japanese. (pp.8-9)

Now say "My name is...". (pp.8-9)

Say "Pleased to meet you, Maeda-san". (pp.8-9)

Japanese has two sets of vocabulary for family members, depending on whether you are talking about your own or someone else's. This lesson concentrates on talking about your own family. As **chichi** means _my father_, **musume** _my daughter_, etc., there is no need for a separate word meaning _my_.

2 **Match and repeat** (5 minutes)

Look at the numbered family members in this scene and match them with the vocabulary list at the side. Read the Japanese words aloud. Now, hide the list with the cover flap and test yourself.

❶ 祖母
 sobo

❷ 祖父
 sofu

❸ 父
 chichi

❹ 母
 haha

❺ 息子
 musuko

❻ 娘
 musume

❶ my grandmother
❷ my grandfather
❸ my father
❻ my daughter
❹ my mother
❺ my son

Conversational tip Japanese distinguishes between little and big sister or brother. You will find all the relevant words in section 4. The word **kyohdai** (siblings) is used to refer to your brothers and sisters as a group: **kyohdai ga yo nin imasu** (I have four siblings).

3 Words to remember: relatives (4 minutes)

The numbers opposite are "general" numerals used for mathematical functions or for money. The Japanese use a system of "classifiers" to count specific things. These vary with the nature of what is being counted, for example, its shape (long and thin, round and flat, etc.). A beginner can get away with using the general numbers, but it's useful to know the classifiers used for people to talk about your family:

一人	hitori	1 person
二人	futari	2 people
三人	san nin	3 people
四人	yo nin	4 people
五人	go nin	5 people
六人	roku nin	6 people
七人	shichi nin	7 people
八人	hachi nin	8 people
九人	kyu nin	9 people
十人	jyu nin	10 people

one	一	ichi
two	二	ni
three	三	san
four	四	shi/yon
five	五	go
six	六	roku
seven	七	shichi/nana
eight	八	hachi
nine	九	kyu
ten	十	jyu
eleven	十一	jyu-ichi
twelve	十二	jyu-ni

4 Words to remember: numbers (5 minutes)

妻
tsuma
my wife

夫
otto
my husband

結婚しています。
kekkon shite imasu
I'm married.

Look at these words and say them aloud. Hide the text on the right with the cover flap and try to remember the Japanese. Check your answers and repeat if necessary. Then practise the phrases below.

my big sister/ my little sister	姉/妹 *ane/imohto*
my big brother/ my little brother	兄/弟 *ani/otohto*
my siblings	兄弟 *kyohdai*
This is my wife.	これは私の妻です。 *kore wa watashi no tsuma desu*
I have four children.	子供が四人います。 *kodomo ga yo nin imasu*
We have two daughters.	娘が二人います。 *musume ga futari imasu*

Say the Japanese for as many members of (your own) family as you can. (pp.10-11)

Say "I have two sons". (pp.10-11)

SHINSEKI
Your relatives

Japanese has more respectful terms when referring to someone else's relatives. *Your mother* is **okahsan**; *your* is understood. Likewise, it's not common to use *his* or *her*, but to specify a name (+ **san**), for example, **kore wa Akkiko-san no otohsan desu** (*This is her [Akiko's] father*).

2 **Words to remember** (5 minutes)

There are different words for referring to family members in Japanese. Here are the more respectful terms for someone else's family.

お母さん *okahsan*	mother
お父さん *otohsan*	father
息子さん *musuko san*	son
娘さん *musume san*	daughter
奥さん *okusan*	wife
ご主人 *goshujin*	husband
子供さん *kodomo san*	children
ご兄弟 *go kyohdai*	siblings

これはお母さんですか？
kore wa okahsan desuka
Is this your mother?

3 **In conversation** (4 minutes)

これはご主人ですか？
kore wa goshujin desuka

Is this your husband?

そうです。そして
これは私の父です。
*sodesu. soshite kore wa
watashi no chichi desu*

That's right. And this is
my father.

子供さんはいますか？
kodomo san wa imasuka

Do you have any children?

Conversational tip Forming a question in Japanese is straightforward. Generally you add the question marker か *ka* to the end of a sentence: *a-re wa musuko san desu* (*That's your son*); *a-re wa musuko san desuka* (*Is that your son?*). In less formal spoken Japanese, the question marker is sometimes dropped: *a-re wa musuko san*.

4 Useful phrases (3 minutes)

Read these phrases aloud several times and try to memorize them. Conceal the Japanese with the cover flap and test yourself.

Do you have any siblings? (formal)	ご兄弟はいらっしゃいますか？ *go kyohdai wa irasshai masuka*
Do you have any siblings? (informal)	兄弟いる？ *kyohdai iru*
Is this your father?	これはお父さんですか？ *kore wa otohsan desuka*
Is that your son? (formal)	あれは息子さんですか？ *a-re wa musuko san desuka*
This is Akiko's daughter.	これは明子さんの娘さんです。 *kore wa Akiko-san no musume san desu*
Is that your little sister? (informal)	あれは妹？ *a-re wa imohto*

5 Say it (2 minutes)

Is this your wife?

Is that your little brother?

Do you have a son? (informal)

This is Akiko's mother.

いいえ、でも妹がいます。
ihe, demo imohto ga imasu

No, but I have a little sister.

1 **Warm up** (1 minute)

Say "See you tomorrow".
(pp.8-9)

Say "I'm married"
(pp.10-11) and
"Is this your wife?"
(pp.12-13)

DESU/GA ARIMASU
To be/there is

The most common verb in Japanese is **desu**, meaning *is*, *are*, or *am*. The u is pronounced only slightly, often making it sound more like **dess**. **Desu** is placed at the end of a sentence and does not change depending on the subject (*I*, *you*, *he*, etc.): **watashi wa Robahto desu** (*I'm Robert*).

2 Useful phrases with desu (2 minutes)

Notice that you'll often find the marker は *wa* or が *ga* after the subject of a sentence. The word order is: subject + *wa/ga* (subject marker) + rest of sentence + *desu*.

私は日本人です。 *watashi wa nihonjin desu*	I'm Japanese.
今10時です。 *ima jyuji desu*	It's ten o'clock.
あなたはお医者 さんですか？ *anata wa oisha san desuka*	Are you a doctor?
明子さんは学生です。 *Akiko-san wa gakusei desu*	Akiko is a student.

Read it It's not as difficult to decipher Japanese script as it may at first appear. The most important thing to appreciate initially is that typical Japanese sentences consist of a mixture of three different character systems:
1. Kanji: Traditional Chinese characters imported into Japanese, e.g. 車 **kuruma** (*car*), 母 **haha** (*my mother*). *Kanji* represent an idea, rather than a particular sound.
2. Hiragana: Japanese characters representing syllables, e.g. で **de**, れ **re**. Hiragana is often used for grammatical words, e.g. です **desu** (*is*), あれ **a-re** (*that*).
3. Katakana: A second syllabary mainly used for foreign loan words, e.g. アメリカ **amerika** (*America*), ケーキ **kehki** (*cake*).

私はイギリス人です。
watashi wa igirisu jin desu
I'm English.

3 Useful phrases: talking about what you have (5 minutes)

An informal and straightforward way to talk about what you have is to use the expression *(ga/wa) arimasu,* literally meaning *there is.* This changes to *(ga/wa) imasu* when talking about people rather than objects.

I have three children.	子供が三人います。 *kodomo ga san nin imasu*
My son has a car.	息子には車があります。 *musuko niwa kuruma ga arimasu*
I have a little sister.	妹がいます。 *imohto ga imasu*
Do you have any children?	子供さんはいますか？ *kodomo san wa imasuka*

名刺があります。
meishi ga arimasu
I have a business card.

4 Negatives (3 minutes)

Negative sentences are made in different ways in Japanese, but sometimes use the negative phrase *arimasen.* Learn these phrases and then test yourself by concealing the answers with the cover flap.

| We're not American. | アメリカ人ではありません。
amerika jin dewa arimasen |
| I don't have a car. | 車がありません。
kuruma ga arimasen |

5 Put into practice (4 minutes)

Join in this conversation. Read the Japanese beside the pictures on the left and then follow the instructions to make your reply. Then test yourself by concealing the answers with the cover flap.

こんばんは。
konbanwa
Good evening.

Say: Good evening. I'm Robert.

こんばんは。私は ロバートです。
konbanwa. watashi wa Robahto desu

どうぞよろしく。
dohzo yoroshiku
Pleased to meet you.

Say: I have a business card.

名刺があります。
meishi ga arimasu

Kotae
Answers (Cover with flap)

FUKUSHU TO KURIKAESH
Review and repeat

1 How many?

❶ 三
san

❷ 九
kyu

❸ 四
shi/yon

❹ 二
ni

❺ 八
hachi

❻ 十
jyu

❼ 五
go

❽ 七
shichi/nana

❾ 六
roku

1 How many? (2 minutes)

Hide the answers with the cover flap. Then say these Japanese numbers aloud. Check you have remembered the Japanese correctly.

2 Hello

❶ こんばんは。
私の名前は...です。
konbanwa. watashi no namae wa...desu

❷ どうぞ、よろしく。
dohzo yoroshiku

❸ 息子が二人います。
子供さんはいますか？
musuko ga futari imasu. kodomo san wa imasuka

❹ さようなら。
sayohnara

2 Hello (4 minutes)

You meet someone in a formal situation. Join in the conversation, replying in Japanese following the English prompts.

konbanwa. watashi no namae wa Maeda Mikiro desu
❶ Answer the greeting and give your name.

kore wa watashi no tsuma desu
❷ Say "Pleased to meet you".

kodomo san wa imasuka
❸ Say "I have two sons. Do you have any children?"

kodomo ga yo nin imasu
❹ Say "Goodbye" formally.

3 **Be or have** (5 minutes)

Fill in the blanks with *desu* (to be) or *arimasu/
imasu* (there is/are used to mean has/have).
Then check you have remembered correctly.

❶ *watashi wa nihonjin* _____

❷ *ani ga* _____

❸ *anata wa gakusei
   san* _____ *ka*

❹ *Sarah-san wa igirisu
   jin* _____

❺ *watashi no namae wa
   Okada* _____

❻ *meishi ga* _____

❼ *kore wa watashi
   no otto* _____

❽ *musume ga
   futari* _____

3 **Be or have**

❶ です
   desu

❷ います
   imasu

❸ です
   desu

❹ です
   desu

❺ です
   desu

❻ あります
   arimasu

❼ です
   desu

❽ います
   imasu

4 **Family** (4 minutes)

Say the Japanese for each of the numbered family
members. Check you have remembered the
Japanese correctly.

❶ my grandmother   ❷ my grandfather   ❸ my father

my daughter ❻   ❺ my son   ❹ my mother

4 **Family**

❶ 祖母
   sobo

❷ 祖父
   sofu

❸ 父
   chichi

❹ 娘
   musume

❺ 息子
   musuko

❻ 母
   haha

KAFE DE
In the café

① **Warm up** (1 minute)

Count up to ten.
(pp.10-11)

Remind yourself how
to say "hello" and
"goodbye". (pp.8-9)

Ask "Do you have
any children?" (pp.14-15)

You will find different types of cafés in
Japan: there are traditional cafés, the
most common of which is called *an-mitsu
kissa*; and Western-style coffee houses,
simply called *kafe* or *kissaten*. These
cafés are very popular, particularly
amongst younger Japanese.

② **Words to remember** (5 minutes)

Look at the words below and say them out aloud a
few times. Conceal the Japanese with the cover flap
and try to remember each one in turn. Practise also
the words on the right.

ココア *kokoah*	hot chocolate
ミルクティー *miruku tih*	tea with milk
お茶 *ocha*	(green) tea
サンドイッチ *sando icchi*	sandwich

紅茶
kohcha
(red) tea

Cultural tip The generic Japanese word for tea is *cha*.
In a regular café, Japanese *green tea* would be called *ocha*,
sencha or *ryokucha*. Western-style tea is known
as *kohcha* (*red tea*).

③ **In conversation** (4 minutes)

コーヒーをお願い
します。
koh-hi o onegai shimasu

A coffee, please.

他にご注文は？
hoka ni gochumon wa

Anything else?

ケーキはありますか？
kehki wa arimasuka

Do you have any cakes?

4 Useful phrases (5 minutes)

Learn these phrases. Read the English under the
pictures and say the phrase in Japanese as shown
on the right. Then cover up the answers on the
right and test yourself.

ケーキ
kehki
cake

コーヒーをお願い
します。
koh-hi o onegai shimasu

A coffee, please.

他にご注文は？
hoka ni gochumon wa

Anything else?

砂糖
satoh
sugar

ケーキもお願いします。
kehki mo onegai shimasu

A cake, too, please.

いくらですか？
ikura desuka

How much is that?

コーヒー
koh-hi
coffee

はい、ございます。
hai, gozaimasu

Yes, certainly.

じゃケーキをお願い
します。いくらですか？
jya kehki o onegai shimasu.
ikura desuka

Then I'd like a cake. How
much is that?

８００円です。
happyaku yen desu

That's 800 yen.

1 Warm up (1 minute)

Say "A coffee, please".
(pp.18-19)

Say "I don't have a car".
(pp.14-15)

Ask "Do you have any
cakes?" (pp.18-19)

RESUTORAN DE
In the restaurant

There are different types of eating places in Japan.
In a bar or café you can find snacks or a light meal.
A **ryohteh** serves traditional Japanese food.
Department stores often house relaxed **resutoran**
on the upper floors, open until about 10pm and
serving both international and Japanese dishes.

2 Words to remember (3 minutes)

Familiarize yourself with these words
and test yourself using the flap.

メニュー *menyu*	menu
ワインリスト *wain risuto*	wine list
スターター *stahtah*	starters
メインコース *mein kohsu*	main courses
デザート *dezahto*	desserts
朝食 *chohshoku*	breakfast
昼食 *chu-shoku*	lunch
夕食 *yu-shoku*	dinner

bowl ❼

❺ spoon

❹ fork   ❻ chopsticks

3 In conversation (4 minutes)

四人用のテーブルは空いて
いますか？
*yonin yoh no tehburu wa
aite imasuka*

Do you have a table
for four?

予約なさっていますか？
yoyaku nasatte imasuka

Do you have a
reservation?

はい。バーカーで
予約しています。
*hai. Barker de yoyaku
shite imasu*

Yes, in the name
of Barker.

4 Match and repeat (5 minutes)

Look at the numbered items in this table setting and match them with the Japanese words on the right. Read the Japanese words aloud. Now, conceal the Japanese with the cover flap and test yourself.

① glass

hand towel **②**

plate **③**

❶ グラス
gurasu

❷ おしぼり
oshibori

❸ 皿
sara

❹ フォーク
forku

❺ スプーン
supuun

❻ おはし
ohashi

❼ ボール
bohru

5 Useful phrases (2 minutes)

Practise these phrases and then test yourself using the cover flap to conceal the Japanese.

What type of sushi do you have?	どんな種類の寿司がありますか？ *don-na shurui no sushi ga arimasuka*
Where can I pay?	どこで払えますか？ *doko de harae masuka*

喫煙席か禁煙席のどちらでしょうか？
kitsu-en seki ka kin-en seki no dochira deshohka

Would you like smoking or non-smoking?

禁煙席をお願いします。
kin-en seki o onegai shimasu

Non-smoking, please.

はい。こちらへどうぞ。
hai. kochira e dohzo

Very well. Here you are.

TABEMONO
Dishes

Say "I'm married" (pp.10-11) and "I'm English". (pp.14-15)

Ask "Do you have any siblings?" (pp.12-13)

Say "A sandwich, please". (pp.18-19)

A typical meal in Japan would consist of rice and miso soup, together with a variety of fish, meat, and vegetable dishes. The meal is served with pickles and other condiments, such as ginger and horseradish. Dessert is usually a selection of fruit. Sweet puddings are not very common.

Cultural tip In restaurants and food halls, *tehshoku* (set menus) are popular, particularly at lunchtime. These consist of a soup, rice, pickles, and other dishes of your choice – all presented on a tray.

2 Match and repeat (4 minutes)

Look at the numbered items and match them to the Japanese words in the panel on the left.

❶ 果物
kudamono

❷ きのこ
kinoko

❸ 米
kome

❹ 野菜
yasai

❺ スープ
supu

❻ 麺類
men rui

❼ 魚
sakana

❽ 肉
niku

❾ シーフード
shifudo

fruit ❶

❷ mushrooms

rice ❸

❺ soup

fish ❼

❽ meat

3 Words to remember: cooking methods (3 minutes)

Familiarize yourself with these words.

fried	揚げた *ageta*
grilled	焼いた *yaita*
roasted	ローストした *rohsuto shita*
boiled	ゆでた *yudeta*
steamed	蒸した *mushita*
raw	生の *nama no*

この魚は生のですか？
kono sakana wa nama no desuka
Is this fish raw?

4 Say it (2 minutes)

What's *Yakitori*?

A beer, please.

Is this fish grilled?

5 Words to remember: drinks (3 minutes)

Familiarize yourself with these words.

water	水 *mizu*
mineral water	ミネラルウォーター *mineraru wohtah*
saki	お酒 *osake*
wine	ワイン *wain*
beer	ビール *bihru*
fruit juice	フルーツジュース *furutsu jyusu*

getables ➍

noodles ➏

6 Useful phrases (2 minutes)

Practise these phrases and then test yourself.

I'm vegetarian.	ベジタリアンです。 *bejitarian desu*
I'm allergic to nuts.	ナッツ類でアレルギー反応を起こします。 *nattsu rui de arerugih hannoh o okoshimasu*
What's Chirinabe?	ちり鍋とは何ですか？ *chirinabe towa nan desuka*

➒ seafood

SHITE KUDASAI
Requests

1 Warm up (1 minute)

What are "breakfast", "lunch", and "dinner" in Japanese? (pp.20-1)

Say "I'm vegetarian" and "What's Sukiyaki?" in Japanese. (pp.22-3)

The simplest way to ask for something in Japanese is to say what you want, followed by *o - onegai shimasu* (*please*). You can use this in almost any situation. However, if you really want to impress, for example in a business situation, you could use the polite formula *itadake masuka*.

2 Basic requests (6 minutes)

Here are some phrases using (*o*) *onegai shimasu* for making basic requests in Japanese. Learn these phrases and then test yourself by using the cover flap.

紅茶をお願いします。 *kohcha o onegai shimasu*	(I'd like) some tea, please.
ケーキをお願いします。 *kehki o onegai shimasu*	(I'd like) a cake, please.
フォークをお願いします。 *forku o onegai shimasu*	(I'd like) a fork, please.
3人用のテーブル をお願いします。 *san nin yoh no tehburu* *o onegai shimasu*	(I'd like) a table for three, please.
メニューをお願いします。 *menyu o onegai shimasu*	(I'd like) the menu, please.
キャンディをお願いします。 *kyandih o onegai shimasu*	(I'd like) some sweets, please.
満タンでお願いします。 *mantan de onegai shimasu*	Fill it up, please. (A full tank, please.)

大和さんおねがい
します。
Yamato-san onegai shimasu
(I'd like) Mr Yamato, please.

Read it Japanese *kanji* ideograms came from Chinese and are still used today. Some *kanji* are simple and resemble the item they describe, like the character for people: 人 (*jin/nin*), but many are quite intricate. The restaurant sign to the left is written in *kanji*. The three vertical characters say *jyun bi chu* (*preparation in progress*) - a polite way of saying *closed*!

3 Polite requests (4 minutes)

In a business situation, you may want to appear ultra-polite, especially if you're talking to someone senior to yourself. Learn these phrases and then test yourself by using the cover flap.

Would you please help me?	手伝っていただけ ますか？ *tetsudatte itadake masuka*
Could I have your signature here, please?	ここにサインを いただけますか？ *koko ni sain o itadake masuka*
Could I have your phone number, please?	電話番号を教えて いただけますか？ *denwa bangoh o oshiete itadake masuka*

4 Put into practice (4 minutes)

Join in this conversation. Read the Japanese beside the pictures on the left and then follow the instructions to make your reply in Japanese. Test yourself by hiding the answers with the cover flap.

こんばんは。予約
なさっていますか？
konbanwa. yoyaku nasatte imasuka

Good evening. Do you have a reservation?

Say: No, but I'd like a table for three.

いいえ、でも３人用の
テーブルをお願いします。
ihe, demo san nin yoh no tehburu o onegai shimasu

お飲物は何になさい
ますか？
onomimono wa nani ni nasai masuka

What would you like to drink?

Say: A beer, please.

ビールをお願い
します。
bihru o onegai shimasu

Kotae
Answers (Cover with flap)

FUKUSHU TO KURIKAESH
Review and repeat

1 What food?

❶ スープ
supu

❷ 野菜
yasai

❸ 魚
sakana

❹ 肉
niku

❺ グラス
gurasu

❻ 米
kome

1 What food? (4 minutes)

Name the numbered items.

❶ soup

❷ vegetables

❸ fish

meat ❹

glass ❺

2 This is my...

❶ これは私の夫
です。
kore wa watashi no otto desu

❷ これは私の娘
です。
kore wa watashi no musume desu

❸ これは私の兄弟
です。
kore wa watashi no kyohdai desu

2 This is my... (4 minutes)

Say these phrases in Japanese.

❶ This is my husband.

❷ This is my daughter.

❸ These are my siblings.

3 I'd like...

❶ ケーキをお願いします。
kehki o onegai shimasu

❷ 砂糖をお願いします。
satoh o onegai shimasu

❸ コーヒーをお願い
します。
koh-hi o onegai shimasu

❹ 紅茶をお願いします。
kohcha o onegai shimasu

3 I'd like... (3 minutes)

Say "I'd like" the following:

❹ tea

cake ❶

sugar ❷

coffee ❸

rice **6**

chopsticks **7**

8 noodles

10 beer

hand towel **9**

1 What food?

7 おはし
ohashi

8 麺類
men rui

9 おしぼり
oshibori

10 ビール
bihru

4 Restaurant (4 minutes)

You arrive at a restaurant. Join in the conversation, replying in Japanese where you see the English prompts.

konbanwa
1 Do you have a table for three?

yoyaku nasatte imasuka
2 Yes, in the name of Barker

kitsu-en seki ka kin-en seki no dochira deshohka
3 Non-smoking, please.

kochira no hoh e dohzo
4 The menu, please.

mochiron gozaimasu
5 Do you have a wine list?

4 Restaurant

1 3人用のテーブルは
空いていますか？
san nin yoh no tehburu wa aite imasuka

2 はい。バーカーで
予約しています。
hai. Barker de yoyaku shite imasu

3 禁煙席をお願い
します。
kin-en seki o onegai shimasu

4 メニューをお願い
します。
menyu o onegai shimasu

5 ワインリストは
ありますか？
wain risuto wa arimasuka

HIZUKE TO TOSHITSUKI
Days and months

1 **Warm up** (1 minute)

How do you say "I have four children"? (pp.10-11)

Now say "We're not English" and "I don't have a car". (pp.14-15)

What is Japanese for "my mother"? (pp.10-11)

The most important holiday of the year in Japan is the three-day New Year Holiday (*shohgatsu sanganichi*). The Japanese usually spend this with family. Christmas is also celebrated, but more often spent with friends.

2 **Words to remember: days of the week** (5 minutes)

Familiarize yourself with these words and test yourself using the flap.

月曜日 *getsuyoh bi*	Monday
火曜日 *kayoh bi*	Tuesday
水曜日 *suiyoh bi*	Wednesday
木曜日 *mokuyoh bi*	Thursday
金曜日 *kin-yoh bi*	Friday
土曜日 *doyoh bi*	Saturday
日曜日 *nichiyoh bi*	Sunday
今日 *kyoh*	today
明日 *ashita*	tomorrow
昨日 *kinoh*	yesterday

明日お会いしましょう。
ashita oai shimashoh
We meet tomorrow.

今日予約があります。
kyoh yoyaku ga arimasu
I have a reservation for today.

3 **Useful phrases: days** (2 minutes)

Learn these phrases and then test yourself using the cover flap.

ミーティングは火曜日では ありません。 *mihtingu wa kayoh bi dewa arimasen*	The meeting isn't on Tuesday.
日曜日に仕事をします。 *nichiyoh bi ni shigoto o shimasu*	I work on Sundays.

4 Words to remember: months of the year (5 minutes)

Japanese months are named simply *1 month, 2 month*, etc.

私たちの記念日は七月です。
watashi tachi no kinenbi wa shichi gatsu desu
Our anniversary is in July.

クリスマスは十二月です。
kurisumasu wa jyu-ni gatsu desu
Christmas is in December.

January	一月	*ichi gatsu*
February	二月	*ni gatsu*
March	三月	*san gatsu*
April	四月	*shi gatsu*
May	五月	*go gatsu*
June	六月	*roku gatsu*
July	七月	*shichi gatsu*
August	八月	*hachi gatsu*
September	九月	*kyu gatsu*
October	十月	*jyu gatsu*
November	十一月	*jyu-ichi gatsu*
December	十二月	*jyu-ni gatsu*
next month	来月	*rai getsu*
last month	先月	*sen getsu*

5 Useful phrases: months (2 minutes)

Learn these phrases and then test yourself using the cover flap.

My children are on holiday in August.
子供たちは八月は休みです。
kodomo tachi wa hachi gatsu wa yasumi desu

My birthday is in June.
私の誕生日は六月です。
watashi no tanjyoh bi wa roku gatsu desu

JIKAN TO SUHJI
Time and numbers

1 **Warm up** (1 minute)

Count in Japanese from
one to twelve. (pp.10-11)

Say "Do you have a
reservation?" (pp.20-1)

Say "The meeting isn't on
Wednesday". (pp.28-9)

When telling the time in Japanese, the hour comes
first, for example, *ichi ji* (*one o'clock*), *ni ji* (*two o'clock*),
etc., followed by the minutes: *go fun* (*five minutes*),
jippun (*ten minutes*). *Mae* is added for times before
the hour: *ni ji nippun mae* (*ten to two*, literally
two o'clock ten minutes before).

2 **Words to remember: time** (4 minutes)

Memorize how to tell the time in Japanese.

1時 *ichi ji*	one o'clock
1時5分 *ichi ji go fun*	five past one
1時15分 *ichi ji jyu-go fun*	quarter past one
1時20分 *ichi ji nijyuppun*	twenty past one
1時半 *ichi ji han*	half past one
1時45分 *ichi ji yonjyu-go fun*	quarter to two ("one forty-five")
2時10分前 *ni ji jippun mae*	ten to two

3 **Useful phrases** (2 minutes)

Learn these phrases and then test yourself using the
cover flap.

今何時ですか？ *ima nanji desuka*	What time is it?
朝食は何時がいい ですか？ *chohshoku wa nanji* *ga iidesuka*	At what time do you want breakfast?
12時に予約を 入れています。 *jyu-ni ji ni yoyaku o* *ireteimasu*	I have a reservation for twelve o'clock.

4 Words to remember: higher numbers (6 minutes)

Japanese numbers are very logical. To count above ten, the individual numbers are simply added together. So 11 is *jyu-ichi* (ten-one), 15 is *jyu-go* (ten-five), etc. Be careful, though, to put the numbers the right way around: *go-jyu* is 50 (five-ten), *nana-jyu* is 70 (seven-ten). Units are added directly after the tens: 68 is *roku-jyu hachi*; 25 is *ni-jyu go*, and so on.

Pay special attention to the number 10,000, which is *man* or *ichi-man*. A million is *hyaku-man* (one hundred-ten thousands).

五千円です。
go-sen yen desu
That's 5,000 yen.

eleven	十一	*jyu-ichi*
twelve	十二	*jyu-ni*
thirteen	十三	*jyu-san*
fourteen	十四	*jyu-shi/jyu-yon*
fifteen	十五	*jyu-go*
sixteen	十六	*jyu-roku*
seventeen	十七	*jyu-shichi*
eighteen	十八	*jyu-hachi*
nineteen	十九	*jyu-kyu*
twenty	二十	*ni-jyu*
thirty	三十	*san-jyu*
forty	四十	*yon-jyu*
fifty	五十	*go-jyu*
sixty	六十	*roku-jyu*
seventy	七十	*nana-jyu*
eighty	八十	*hachi-jyu*
ninety	九十	*kyu-jyu*
hundred	百	*hyaku*
three hundred	三百	*san-byaku*
thousand	千	*sen*
ten thousand	一万	*ichi-man*
two hundred thousand	二十万	*ni-jyu-man*
one million	百万	*hyaku-man*

5 Say it (2 minutes)

twenty-five

ninety-two

two hundred

twenty thousand

five to ten

half past eleven

That's 700 yen.

APO/(GO)YOYAKU
Appointments

1 **Warm up** (1 minute)

Say the days of the week.
(pp.28-9)

Say "three o'clock".
(pp.30-1)

What's the Japanese for
"today", "tomorrow", and
"yesterday"? (pp.28-9)

The Japanese are keen to find out about the status of someone they meet for the first time. This is in order to judge the level of respect due and appropriate formality of the language. The most common way of establishing status is by the virtually obligatory exchange of *business cards* (**meishi**).

2 **Useful phrases** (5 minutes)

Learn these phrases and then test yourself.

明日お会い しましょうか？ *ashita oai shimashohka*	Shall we meet tomorrow?
どなたとですか？ *donata to desuka*	With whom? (formal)
いつお暇ですか？ *itsu ohima desuka*	When are you free?
すみません。 その日は忙しいです。 *sumimasen. sonohi wa isogashih desu*	Sorry. I'm busy that day.
木曜日はどうですか？ *mokuyoh bi wa doh desuka*	How about Thursday?
大丈夫です。 *daijyohbu desu*	That's good for me.

ようこそ。
yohkoso
Welcome.

3 **In conversation** (4 minutes)

こんにちは。アポを入れて いるのですが。
konnichiwa. apo o ireteiru no desuga

Hello. I have an appointment.

どなたとですか？
donata to desuka

With whom?

田中さんとです。
Tanaka-san to desu

With Mr Tanaka.

4 Put into practice (5 minutes)

Practise these phrases. Then cover up the text on the right and say the
answering part of the dialogue in Japanese. Check your answers
and repeat if necessary.

木曜日にお会いしましょうか？
*mokuyoh bi ni
oai shimashohka*

Shall we meet on Thursday?

Say: Sorry. I'm busy
that day.

すみません。
その日は忙しいです。
*sumimasen. sonohi wa
isogashih desu*

いつお暇ですか？
itsu ohima desuka

When are you free?

Say: On Tuesday in
the afternoon.

火曜日の午後なら空いて
います。
*kayoh bi no gogo nara
aite imasu*

私も大丈夫です。
watashi mo daijyobu desu

That's good for me, too.

Ask: At what time?

何時がよろしいですか？
nanji ga yoroshih desuka

Read it It's useful to recognize some common Japanese signs you might see around a
building. The signs below are a combination of two *kanji* characters. *Madoguchi* means
literally *window mouth*!

 uketsuke
(reception)

 madoguchi
(information desk)

そうですか。
何時のご予約ですか？
*sohdesuka. nanji no
goyoyaku desuka*

Very good. What time is
the appointment?

3時ですが。
san ji desuga

At three o'clock.

どうぞ、おかけください。
dohzo okake kudasai

Take a seat, please.

1　Warm up (1 minute)

How do you say "sorry"? (pp.32-3)

Ask "Shall we meet tomorrow?" (pp.32-3)

Say "(I'd like) a cake, please". (pp.24-5)

DENWA DE
On the telephone

The Japanese answer the telephone with **moshi moshi** (hello), rather than **konnichiwa**. Public telephones are usually green. Almost all work with *phonecards* (**tereka**) available from most stores. International calls can be difficult from mobiles because of the different network specifications.

2　Match and repeat (6 minutes)

Match the numbered items to the Japanese in the panel below and test yourself.

❶ チャージャー
chahjyah

❷ 留守番電話
rusuban denwa

❸ 電話
denwa

❹ テレカ
tereka

❺ 携帯
kehtai

❻ イヤフォン
iyafon

❸ telephone
❶ charger
earphones ❻
❺ mobile

3　In conversation (4 minutes)

もしもし、ジャパニーズ コネクションです。
moshi moshi, japanihzu konekushon desu

Hello. This is Japanese Connection.

もしもし、岡田さんをお願いします。
moshi moshi, Okada-san o onegai shimasu

Hello. (I'd like to speak to) Ms Okada, please.

どちら様ですか？
dochira sama desuka

Who's speaking?

4 Useful phrases (4 minutes)

Practise these phrases. Then test yourself using the cover flap.

テレカをください。
tereka o kudasai
I'd like a phonecard.

外線につなげてください。
gaisen ni tsunagete kudasai

Please connect me to an outside line.

② answering machine

岡田さんをお願いします。
Okada-san o onegai shimasu

(I'd like to speak to) Mr/Ms Okada, please.

メッセージを伝えて
いただけますか？
messehji o tsutaete itadake masuka

Can I leave a message?

④ phonecard

すみません、
番号を間違えました。
sumimasen, bangoh o machigae mashita

Sorry, I have the wrong number.

ゴープレス・プリンターの前
田美樹朗と申します。
Gopress purintah no Maeda Mikiro to mohshimasu

Maeda Mikiro of Gopress Printers.

すみません。ただ今
話し中です。
sumimasen. tadaima hanashichu desu

I'm sorry. The line is busy.

岡田さんの方から連絡
いただけますか？
Okada-san no hokara renraku itadake masuka

Can Ms Okada call me back, please?

Kotae
Answers (Cover with flap)

FUKUSHU TO KURIKAESHI
Review and repeat

1 Sums

❶ 十六
jyu-roku

❷ 三十九
san-jyu kyu

❸ 五十三
go-jyu san

❹ 七十八
nana-jyu hachi

❺ 九十九
kyu-jyu kyu

❻ 十七
jyu-shichi

1 Sums (4 minutes)

Say the answers to these sums out loud in Japanese. Then check you have remembered correctly.

❶ $10 + 6 = ?$

❷ $14 + 25 = ?$

❸ $66 - 13 = ?$

❹ $40 + 38 = ?$

❺ $90 + 9 = ?$

❻ $20 - 3 = ?$

3 Telephones (3 minutes)

What are the numbered items in Japanese?

❶ mobile

phonecard ❸

2 To want

❶ します
shimasu

❷ お願い
onegai

❸ ますか
masuka

❹ いただけ
itadake

❺ お願い
onegai

❻ 人
nin

2 To want (3 minutes)

Fill the gaps in these requests with the correct word.

❶ Yamato-san onegai _____ .

❷ kyandih o _____ shimasu.

❸ koko ni sain o itadake _____ .

❹ tetsudatte _____ masuka.

❺ bihru o _____ shimasu.

❻ san _____ yoh no tehburu o onegai shimasu.

Kotae
Answers (Cover with flap)

3 Telephones

❶ 携帯
kehtai

❷ 留守番電話
rusuban denwa

❸ テレカ
tereka

❹ 電話
denwa

❺ イヤフォン
iyafon

telephone ❹

answering ❷
machine

❺ earphones

---

4 When? (2 minutes)

What do these sentences mean?

❶ *dewa mata ashita*

❷ *doyoh bi ni shigoto o shimasu*

❸ *watashi no tanjyoh bi wa go gatsu desu*

❹ *kyoh yoyaku ga arimasu*

4 When?

❶ *See you tomorrow.*

❷ *I work on Saturday.*

❸ *My birthday is in May.*

❹ *I have a reservation for today.*

---

5 Time (3 minutes)

Say these times in Japanese.

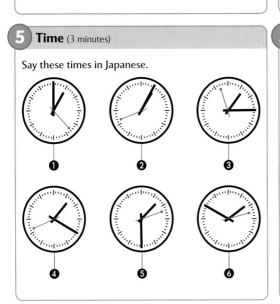

❶ ❷ ❸

❹ ❺ ❻

5 Time

❶ 1時
ichi ji

❷ 1時5分
ichi ji go fun

❸ 1時15分
ichi ji jyu-go fun

❹ 1時20分
ichi ji nijyuppun

❺ 1時半
ichi ji han

❻ 2時10分前
ni ji jippun mae

Warm up (1 minute)

Count to 100 in tens.
(pp.10-11 and pp.30-1)

Ask "What time is it?"
(pp.30-1)

Say "half past one".
(pp.30-1)

EKI DE
At the station

Japan is famous for its clean, fast, and reliable train services. The network covers the entire country and there are different types of train: local **futsu** and **kaisoku** commuter trains, **kyuko** and **tokkyu** express trains; and the famous **shinkansen** high-speed intercity "bullet" trains.

Words to remember (3 minutes)

Learn these words and then test yourself.

駅 *eki*	station
電車 *densha*	train
プラットホーム *purattohohmu*	platform
チケット *chiketto*	ticket
片道 *katamichi*	single
往復 *ohfuku*	return
一等 / 二等車 *ittoh/nitoh sha*	first/second class
乗り換え *norikae*	change (trains)

改札口
kaisatsu guchi
ticket barrier

サイン
sain
sign

乗客
jyohkyaku
passenger

この駅は混んでいます。
kono eki wa konde imasu
This station is crowded.

In conversation (4 minutes)

京都行きを二枚おねがいします。
Kyoto iki o nimai onegai shimasu

Two to Kyoto, please.

往復ですか？
ohfuku desuka

Is that return?

はい。席の予約が必要ですか？
hai. seki no yoyaku ga hitsuyo desuka

Yes. Do I need to make seat reservations?

4 Useful phrases (5 minutes)

大阪への電車は遅れて
います。
*Osaka eno densha wa
okurete imasu*
The train for Osaka is late.

Learn these phrases and then test yourself using
the cover flap.

How much is a ticket to Nagasaki?	長崎行きのチケット はいくらですか？ *Nagasaki iki no chiketto wa ikura desuka*
Can I use a credit card?	クレジットカード が使えますか？ *kurejitto kahdo ga tsukae masuka*
Do I have to change?	乗り換えしなければ いけませんか？ *norikae shinakereba ikemasenka*
Which platform does the train leave from?	電車はどのプラットホーム から発車しますか？ *densha wa dono purattohohmu kara hassha shimasuka*
What time does the train leave?	電車は何時に発車しますか？ *densha wa nanji ni hassha shimasuka*

5 Say it (2 minutes)

This train is crowded.

How much is a ticket
to Osaka?

Cultural tip You might need to buy your rail tickets
from machines. These machines can be complicated to
navigate and you may need someone
to help you. But all the destinations are
written in phonetic *katakana* characters,
as well as *kanji*, to help children (and
foreigners) to read the signs.

いいえ。一万円に
なります。
*ihe. ichiman-yen
ni narimasu*

No. That's 10,000 yen.

クレジットカード
が使えますか？
*kurejitto kahdo ga
tsukae masuka*

Can I use a credit card?

はい。電車はプラット
ホーム1番から発車します。
*hai. densha wa
purattohohmu ichiban
kara hassha shimasu*

Yes. The train leaves
from platform one.

IKU/NORU
To go and to take

1 Warm up (1 minute)

How do you say
"train"? (pp.38-9)

What are "tomorrow"
and "yesterday" in
Japanese? (pp.28-9)

Count from 10 to 20.
(pp.30-1)

Iku (to go) and *noru* (to take) are essential verbs
you will need as you find your way around. Japanese
verbs do not change according to the subject, but
do have different endings for the tense (present/past)
or mood (requesting/wanting, etc.). Note also that
the verb usually comes at the end of a sentence.

2 Iku/noru: to go and to take (6 minutes)

The basic verb (*iku/noru*) can be used by itself, but often an ending is added. The
present tense of Japanese verbs generally ends in *-masu*: *ikimasu* (go, am/are/is
going) and the negative in *-masen*: *ikemasen* (don't go, am not/aren't/isn't going).
The "wanting" mood ends in *-tai*: *noritai* (want to take).

どこ行くの？ *doko iku no*	Where are you going? (informal)
どこに行かれるの ですか？ *doko ni ikareru no desuka*	Where are you going? (formal)
今日は自転車に 乗ります。 *kyoh wa jitensha ni norimasu*	I'm taking my bicycle today.
バスで仕事に 行きます。 *basu de shigoto ni ikimasu*	I go to work by bus.
タクシーでは仕事に 行きません。 *takushih dewa shigotoni ikimasen*	I don't go to work by taxi.
電車に乗りたい です。 *densha ni noritai desu*	I want to take the train.

富士山に行きます。
fujisan ni ikimasu
I'm going to Mount Fuji.

Cultural tip Taxis in Japan are often yellow or green. There's usually a light
at the bottom right of the windscreen: green for occupied and red for available.
The taxis are usually scrupulously clean – drivers even wear white gloves. Back
doors are remote-controlled by the driver, so be careful
you don't get knocked over as you reach for the
handle. Tips are not usual.

3 Past and future (6 minutes)

The ending -*mashita* shows a verb is in the past: *norimashita* (took), *ikimashita* (went). There is no special form for the future. Instead, the present tense can be used with a time indicator, e.g. *ashita* (tomorrow).

タクシーに乗りました。
takushih ni norimashita

I took a taxi.

富士山に電車で行きました。
fujisan ni densha de ikimashita

I went to Mount Fuji by train.

明日地下鉄に乗ります。
ashita chikatetsu ni norimasu

I'll take the underground tomorrow.

明日バスで仕事に行きます。
ashita basu de shigoto ni ikimasu

I'll go to work by bus tomorrow.

4 Put into practice (2 minutes)

Cover the text on the right and complete the dialogue in Japanese.

どこに行かれるのですか？   駅に行きます。
doko ni ikareru no desuka   *eki ni ikimasu*

Where are you going?

Say: I'm going to the station.

地下鉄に乗りたい   いいえ、バスに乗り
ですか？   たいです。
chikatetsu ni noritai desuka   *ihe, basu ni noritai desu*

Do you want to take the underground?

Say: No, I want to take the bus.

三十四番のバス   どうもありがとう
ですよ。   ございます。
san-jyu yon ban no   *dohmo arigatoh*
basu desuyo   *gozaimasu*

That'll be bus number 34.

Say: Thank you very much.

1 Warm up (1 minute)

Say "I want to go to the station". (pp.40-1)

Ask "Where are you going?" (pp.40-1)

What's 45 in Japanese? (pp.30-1)

TAKUSHIH, BASU, CHIKATETSU
Taxi, bus, and underground

On buses you generally take a ticket from a machine as you get on. At the end of your journey, a chart will indicate how much you have to pay.

2 Words to remember (4 minutes)

Familiarize yourself with these words.

バス *basu*	bus
タクシー *takushih*	taxi
地下鉄 *chikatetsu*	underground
バス停 *basu teh*	bus station
タクシー乗り場 *takushih noriba*	taxi rank
地下鉄の駅 *chikatetsu no eki*	underground station
運賃 *unchin*	fare
線 *sen*	line/route

８８番のバスはここで
停まりますか？
*hachijyu-hachi ban no basu
wa kokode tomarimasuka*
Does the number 88
stop here?

3 In conversation: taxi (2 minutes)

秋葉原までお願い
します。
*Akihabara ma-de
onegai shimasu*

To Akihabara, please.

わかりました。
wakarimashita

Very well.

ここで降ろしてください。
kokode oroshite kudasai

Can you drop me
here, please?

4 Useful phrases (4 minutes)

Learn these phrases and then test yourself using the cover flap.

A taxi to Ginza, please.	銀座までのタクシーをお願いします。 *Ginza ma-de no takushih o onegai shimasu*
What time is the next bus to the airport?	空港行きの次のバスは何時ですか？ *ku-koh iki no tsugi no basu wa nanji desuka*
How do you get to Asakusa?	浅草にはどうやって行けばいいですか？ *Asakusa niwa dohyatte ikeba iidesuka*
Please wait for me.	ちょっと待ってください。 *chotto matte kudasai*

Cultural tip Tokyo, Osaka, and other major cities have extensive and efficient metro systems. The different *lines* (**sen**) have names such as **yamanote-sen** (*a circular line which links the network*). Fares vary depending on distance.

東京メトロ
Tokyo Metro

5 Say it (2 minutes)

To the station, please.

A taxi to the airport, please.

How do you get to Akihabara?

6 In conversation: bus (2 minutes)

博物館へ行きますか？
hakubutsu kan e ikimasuka

Do you go to
the museum?

はい。あまり遠くないですよ。
hai. amari tohku naidesuyo

Yes. It's not very far.

どこでおりるか教えてもらえますか？
doko de oriru ka oshiete mora-e masuka

Can you tell me when
to get off?

DOHRO DE
On the road

Gairaigo is a special term used to refer to the many foreign words imported into Japanese, mainly from English. In some areas of life, such as modern machinery and computers, *gairaigo* is dominant. Pay attention, though, to the particularly Japanese way of pronouncing the words.

1 Warm up (1 minute)

How do you say "A coffee, please"? (pp.14-15)

Say "my father", "my sister", and "my parents". (pp.12-13)

Say "I'm going to Ginza". (pp.40-1)

2 Match and repeat (4 minutes)

Match the numbered items to the list below, then test yourself.

❶ フロントガラス
furonto garasu

❷ ボンネット
bon-netto

❸ バンパー
banpah

❹ タイヤ
taiya

❺ ヘッドライト
heddo raito

❻ ドア
doa

❼ 車輪
shahrin

❽ トランク
toranku

❾ サイドミラー
saido mirah

Cultural tip Japan is one of the few countries that drives on the left, as does the UK. Many motorways are toll roads and can be expensive.

❶ windscreen
❷ bonnet
bumper ❸
❹ tyre
❺ headlights

3 Road signs (2 minutes)

一方通行
ippoh tsu-koh

One way

徐行
jyokoh

Proceed slowly

最低速度
saiteh sokudo

Minimum speed limit

4 Useful phrases (4 minutes)

Learn these phrases and then test yourself using the cover flap.

The engine won't start.	エンジンがかかり ません。 *enjin ga kakari masen*
Fill it up, please. (A full tank, please.)	満タンお願いします。 *mantan onegai shimasu*

5 Say it (1 minute)

Diesel, please.

The car won't start.

9 wing mirror

8 boot

6 door

7 wheel

6 Words to remember (3 minutes)

Familiarize yourself with these words then test yourself using the flap.

driving licence	運転免許証	*unten menkyosho*
petrol	ガソリン	*gasorin*
diesel	ディーゼル	*dihzeru*
oil	オイル	*oiru*
engine	エンジン	*enjin*
flat tyre	パンク	*panku*

Read it Road signs are often in Japanese characters only. If you're driving, familiarize yourself with the Japanese script for your destination, as well as the more common signs, such as 止まれ *tomare* (stop).

止まれ
tomare

Stop

進入禁止
shin-nyu kinshi

No entry

駐車禁止
chu-sha kinshi

No parking

Kotae
Answers (Cover with flap)

FUKUSHU TO KURIKAESH
Review and repeat

1 Transport

❶ バス
basu

❷ タクシー
takushih

❸ 車
kuruma

❹ 自転車
jitensha

❺ 地下鉄
chikatetsu

1 Transport (3 minutes)

Name these forms of transport in Japanese.

❶ bus

taxi ❷

2 Go and take

❶ 行きます
ikimasu

❷ 乗りたい
noritai

❸ 行く
iku

❹ 行かれる
ikareru

❺ 乗ります
norimasu

❻ 乗りました
norimashita

2 Go and take (4 minutes)

Use the correct form of the verb in brackets to fill the gaps.

❶ *fujisan ni _____.* *(iku)*

❷ *densha ni _____ desu.* *(noru)*

❸ *doko _____ no.* *(iku)*

❹ *doko ni _____ no desuka.* *(iku)*

❺ *ashita chikatetsu ni _____.* *(noru)*

❻ *kinoh takushih ni _____.* *(noru)*

3 car

4 bicycle

underground **5**

東京メトロ
Tokyo Metro

3 Questions
(4 minutes)

How do you ask these questions in Japanese?

❶ "Do you have any cakes?"

❷ "Do you have any children?"

❸ "What time is it?"

❹ "Do you go to the station?"

❺ "Where are you going?" (informal)

❻ "Can I use a credit card?"

3 Questions

❶ ケーキはありますか？
kehki wa arimasuka

❷ 子供さんはいますか？
kodomo san wa imasuka

❸ 今何時ですか？
ima nanji desuka

❹ 駅へ行きますか？
eki e ikimasuka

❺ どこ行くの？
doko iku no

❻ クレジットカードが使えますか？
kurejitto kahdo ga tsukae masuka

4 Tickets (4 minutes)

You're buying tickets at a train station. Join in the conversation, replying in Japanese following the numbered English prompts.

konnichiwa
❶ Two to Osaka, please.

ohfuku desuka
❷ No. Single, please.

ichiman-yen ni narimasu
❸ What time does the train leave?

ni ji jippun mae desu
❹ Which platform does the train leave from?

purattohohmu wa ichiban desu
❺ Thank you very much.

4 Tickets

❶ 大阪行きを二枚お願いします。
Osaka iki o nimai onegai shimasu

❷ いいえ。片道をお願いします。
ihe. katamichi o onegai shimasu

❸ 電車は何時に発車しますか？
densha wa nanji ni hassha shimasuka

❹ 電車はどのプラットホームから発車しますか？
densha wa dono purattohohmu kara hassha shimasuka

❺ どうもありがとうございます。
dohmo arigato gozaimasu

1 **Warm up** (1 minute)

Ask "Do you go to the museum?" (pp.42-3)

What are "station" and "ticket" in Japanese? (pp.38-9)

MACHI DE
About town

To talk about features or facilities, you can use the phrases *ga/wa arimasu* (*there is/are*) and *ga/wa arimasen* (*there isn't/aren't*). Notice the word order is the opposite to English: *hashi no chikaku ni suimingu pu-ru ga arimasu* = bridge/near to/swimming pool/there is (*There's a swimming pool near the bridge*).

2 **Match and repeat** (4 minutes)

Match the numbered locations to the words in the panel.

❶ 横断歩道
ohdan hodoh

❷ 橋
hashi

❸ デパート
depahto

❹ 駐車場
chusha jyo

❺ 噴水
funsui

❻ 広場
hiroba

❼ 博物館
hakubutsu kan

❽ 映画館
eiga kan

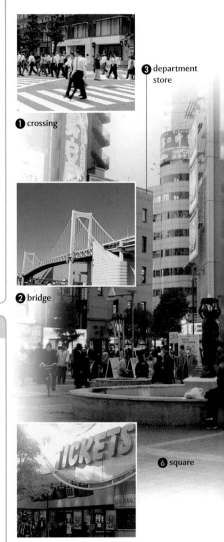

❸ department store

❶ crossing

❷ bridge

❻ square

❽ cinema

3 **Words to remember** (4 minutes)

Familiarize yourself with these words and test yourself using the cover flap.

ガソリンスタンド *gasorin sutando*	petrol station
観光案内所 *kankoh an-naijyo*	tourist information centre
スイミングプール *suimingu pu-ru*	swimming pool
ネットカフェ *netto kafeh*	internet café

4 Useful phrases (4 minutes)

Learn these phrases and then test yourself using the cover flap.

Is there a museum in town?	街に博物館が ありますか？ *machi ni hakubutsu kan ga arimasuka*
Is it far from here?	ここから遠い ですか？ *koko kara toh-i desuka*
There's a swimming pool near the bridge.	橋の近くにスイミング プールがあります。 *hashi no chikaku ni suimingu pu-ru ga arimasu*
There isn't a tourist information centre.	観光案内所はありません。 *kankoh an-naijyo wa arimasen*

寺は街の真ん中にあります。
*tera wa machi no man-naka
ni arimasu*
The temple is in the
centre of town.

5 Put into practice (2 minutes)

Join in this conversation. Read the Japanese on the left and follow the instructions to make your reply. Then test yourself by concealing the answers with the cover flap.

4 car park

5 fountain

どうしました？
doh shimashita

Is everything OK?

Ask: Is there an internet café nearby?

この近くにネットカフェは
ありますか？
*kono chikaku ni netto kafe
wa arimasuka*

いいえ、でも観光案内所は
あります。
*ihe, demo kankoh an-
naijyo wa arimasu*

No, but there's a tourist information centre.

Ask: Is it far from here?

ここから遠い
ですか？
koko kara toh-i desuka

駅の近くです。
eki no chikaku desu

It's near the station.

Say: Thank you.

ありがとうございます。
arigatoh gozaimasu

7 museum

1 Warm up (1 minute)

How do you say "bridge" and "fountain"? (pp.48-9)

Ask "Is it far from here?" (pp.48-9)

Ask "Is there a museum in town?" (pp.48-9)

MICHI O KIKU
Asking directions

Finding your way around town in Japan can be confusing, so it's a good idea to learn how to ask for and understand directions. Remember that Japanese word order is different from English: **kado o hidari ni magatte kudasai** = corner at/left towards/turn/please (*Turn left at the corner*).

2 Useful phrases (4 minutes)

Practise these phrases and then test yourself.

左 / 右に曲がってください。 *hidari/migi ni magatte kudasai*	(Please) turn left/right.
左に / 右に。 *hidari ni/migi ni*	On the left/on the right.
まっすぐ。 *massugu*	Straight on.
寺にはどうやって行けばいいですか？ *tera niwa dohyatte ikeba iidesuka*	How do I get to the temple?
左側の最初の道。 *hidari gawa no saisho no michi*	First street on the left.
右の二番目の道。 *migi no ni-banme no michi*	Second street on the right.

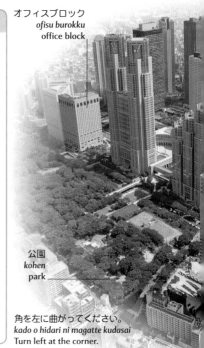

オフィスブロック
ofisu burokku
office block

公園
kohen
park

角を左に曲がってください。
kado o hidari ni magatte kudasai
Turn left at the corner.

3 In conversation (4 minutes)

この街にレストランはありますか？
kono machi ni resutoran wa arimasuka

Is there a restaurant in town?

はい。駅の近くにあります。
hai. eki no chikaku ni arimasu

Yes, near the station.

駅にはどうやって行けばいいですか？
eki niwa dohyatte ikeba iidesuka

How do I get to the station?

4 Words to remember (4 minutes)

道に迷いました。
michi ni mayoi mashita
I'm lost.

Familiarize yourself with these words and test yourself using the flap.

traffic lights	信号	*shingoh*
corner	角	*kado*
street	道	*michi*
road	道路	*dohro*
map	地図	*chizu*
flyover	立体交差	*rittai kohsa*
opposite	反対側	*hantai gawa*
at the end of the street	道の終わりに	*michi no owari ni*

ここはどこですか？
koko wa doko desuka
Where are we?

5 Say it (2 minutes)

Turn right at the traffic lights.

Turn left at the station.

It's about ten minutes.

信号を左に曲がって
ください。
*shingoh o hidari ni
magatte kudasai*

Turn left at the traffic lights.

遠いですか？
toh-i desuka

Is it far?

いいえ、5分くらいです。
ihe, go fun kurai desu

No, it's about
five minutes.

KANKOH
Sightseeing

1 Warm up (1 minute)

Say the days of the week in Japanese. (pp.28-9)

How do you say "six o'clock"? (pp.30-1)

Ask "What time is it?" (pp.30-1)

Japanese shops open late, closing around 10 or 11pm. The main closing days for tourist sights are Sunday or Monday. However, urban Japan is a 24/7 society and you will generally find a few *konbini* (abbreviated from *convenience stores*) and cafés open whatever the time of day or night.

2 Words to remember (4 minutes)

Familiarize yourself with these words and test yourself using the flap.

ガイドブック *gaido bukku*	guidebook
入場無料 *nyu-jyo muryoh*	free entrance
開館時間 *kaikan jikan*	opening times (museums, libraries)
営業時間 *eigyoh jikan*	opening times (shops, restaurants)
休日 *kyu jitsu*	public holiday

ガイド付きツアー
gaido tsuki tsuah
guided tour

Cultural tip There are many unusual free attractions in Japan. These include beer, sake, and fishcake museums, wine cellars, food factories, galleries, electronics and cosmetics showrooms, and even television and film studios.

3 In conversation (3 minutes)

今日の午後は開いて
いますか？
*kyoh no koko wa aite
imasuka*

Do you open this afternoon?

はい、でも六時には
閉まります。
*hai, demo roku ji niwa
shimari masu*

Yes, but we close at six o'clock.

車いすは使えますか？
*kurumaisu wa tsukae
masuka*

Is wheelchair access possible?

4 Useful phrases (3 minutes)

Learn these phrases and then test yourself using the cover flap.

What time do you open?	何時に開きますか？ *nanji ni akimasuka*
What time does the shop close?	店は何時に閉まりますか？ *mise wa nanji ni shimari masuka*
Is wheelchair access possible?	車いすは使えますか？ *kurumaisu wa tsukae masuka*

5 Put into practice (4 minutes)

Cover the text on the right and complete the dialogue in Japanese.

すみません。博物館は閉館しました。
sumimasen. hakubutsu kan wa heikan shimashita

Sorry. The museum is closed.

Ask: Do you open on Sundays?

日曜日はオープンしていますか？
nichiyo bi wa ohpun shite imasuka

はい、でも早く閉館します。
hai, demo hayaku heikan shimasu

Yes, but we close early.

Ask: At what time?

何時にですか？
nanji ni desuka

はい。あちらにエレベーターがあります。
hai. achira ni erebehtah ga arimasu

Yes, there's a lift over there.

ありがとう。チケットを四枚お願いします。
arigatoh. chiketto o yonmai onegai shimasu

Thank you. I'd like four tickets.

どうぞ。ガイドブックは無料です。
dohzo. gaido bukku wa muryoh desu

Here you are. The guidebook is free.

KU-KOH DE
At the airport

1 **Warm up** (1 minute)

Say "Would you please help me?" (pp.24-5)

What's the Japanese for "ticket"? (pp.38-9)

Say "I'm going to Osaka". (pp.40-1)

International flights arrive at Tokyo's Narita airport and an extensive network of internal flights operate out of the domestic Haneda airport. Although the airport environment is largely universal, it is sometimes useful to be able to understand key words and phrases in Japanese.

2 **Words to remember** (4 minutes)

Familiarize yourself with these words and test yourself using the flap.

チェックイン *chekku in*	check-in
出発 *shuppatsu*	departures
到着 *tohchaku*	arrivals
税関 *zeikan*	customs
入国審査／出国審査 *nyu-koku shinsa/ shukkoku shinsa*	passport control (entering/leaving Japan)
ターミナル *tahminaru*	terminal
搭乗口 *tohjyoh guchi*	gate
…便 *bin*	flight number...

香港行きの飛行機は
どこの搭乗口ですか？
*honkon iki no hikohki
wa doko no tohjyoh
guchi desuka*
Which gate is the flight
to Hong Kong?

3 **Useful phrases** (3 minutes)

Learn these phrases and then test yourself using the cover flap.

ロンドンからの飛行機 は予定通りですか？ *Rondon kara no hikohki wa yotei dohri desuka*	Is the flight from London on time?
荷物が見つかり ません。 *nimotsu ga mitsukari masen*	I can't find my baggage.
京都への飛行機は 遅れています。 *Kyoto eno hikohki wa okurete imasu*	The flight to Kyoto is delayed.

4 Put into practice (3 minutes)

Join in this conversation. Read the Japanese on the left and follow the instructions to make your reply. Then test yourself by concealing the answers with the cover flap.

次の方どうぞ。
tsugi no kata dohzo

Next, please.

Ask: Is the flight to Kyoto on time?

京都への飛行機は予定通りですか？
Kyoto eno hikohki wa yotei dohri desuka

はい。予定通りです。
hai. yotei dohri desu

Yes, it's on time.

Ask: Which gate is it?

どの搭乗口ですか？
dono tohjyoh guchi desuka

5 Match and repeat (4 minutes)

boarding **❶**
pass

ticket **❷**

passport **❸**

❹ suitcase   **❺** trolley

Match the numbered items to the Japanese words in the panel.

❶ 搭乗券
tohjyoh ken

❷ チケット
chiketto

❸ パスポート
pasupohto

❹ スーツケース
su-tsu kehsu

❺ カート
kahto

空港 *ku-koh*
airport

Read it Here's another example of two *kanji* characters combining to make a separate meaning: 空 (*ku*, sky) + 港 (*koh*, port).

Kotae
Answers (Cover with flap)

FUKUSHU TO KURIKAESHI
Review and repeat

1 Places

❶ 博物館
hakubutsu kan

❷ 横断歩道
ohdan hodoh

❸ 橋
hashi

❹ 寺
tera

❺ 駐車場
chusha jyo

❻ 映画館
eiga kan

❼ 広場
hiroba

1 Places (4 minutes)

Name the numbered places in Japanese.

❶ museum　❷ crossing　❸ bridge

❹ temple　❺ car park

❻ cinema

❼ square

2 Car parts

❶ フロントガラス
furonto garasu

❷ ヘッドライト
heddo raito

❸ バンパー
banpah

❹ ドア
doa

❺ タイヤ
taiya

2 Car parts (3 minutes)

Name these car parts in Japanese.

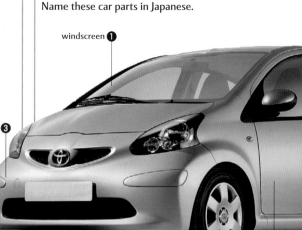

windscreen ❶

bumper ❸

tyre ❺

❹ door

3 Translation (4 minutes)

What do these Japanese phrases mean?

❶ hidari ni magatte kudasai

❷ kono machi ni hakubutsu kan wa arimasuka

❸ mantan de onegai shimasu

❹ koko wa doko desuka

❺ hashi no chikaku ni suimingu puhru ga arimasu

❻ nanji ni akimasuka

❼ chiketto o yonmai onegai shimasu

3 Translation

❶ (Please) turn left.

❷ Is there a museum in town?

❸ Fill it up, please.

❹ Where are we?

❺ There's a swimming pool near the bridge.

❻ What time do you open?

❼ I'd like four tickets.

❷ headlight

4 Directions (4 minutes)

Ask how to get to these places:

❶ temple
❷ station
❸ internet café
❹ cinema

4 Directions

❶ 寺にはどうやって
行けばいいですか？
*tera niwa dohyatte
ikeba iidesuka*

❷ 駅にはどうやって
行けばいいですか？
*eki niwa dohyatte
ikeba iidesuka*

❸ ネットカフェにはどう
やって行けば
いいですか？
*netto kafeh niwa
dohyatte ikeba
iidesuka*

❹ 映画館にはどう
やって行けばいいで
すか？
*eiga kan niwa
dohyatte ikeba
iidesuka*

1 Warm up (1 minute)

Ask "How much is that?" (pp.18-19)

What are "breakfast", "lunch", and "dinner"? (pp.20-1)

What are "three", "four", "five", and "six"? (pp.10-11)

HEYA NO YOYAKU
Booking a room

Japan has a large number of international hotels as well as the traditional Japanese inns (see pp.62-3). *Rabuhoteru* (*love hotels*) rentable by the hour are best avoided. The famous tubular *kapuseruhoteru* (*capsule hotels*) are also available in major cities, but aren't suitable for the claustrophobic.

2 Useful phrases (3 minutes)

Practise these phrases and then test yourself by concealing the Japanese on the left with the cover flap.

朝食込みですか？
chohshoku komi desuka

Is breakfast included?

部屋からインターネットに
アクセスできますか？
*heya kara intahnetto ni
akusesu dekimasuka*

Does the room have internet access?

ルームサービス
はありますか？
*ru-mu sahbisu
wa arimasuka*

Is there room service?

チェックアウトは
何時ですか？
*chekkuauto wa
nanji desuka*

What time is check out?

3 In conversation (5 minutes)

空いている部屋は
ありますか？
*aiteiru heya wa
arimasuka*

Do you have
any rooms?

はい。ダブルルーム
がございます。
*hai. daburu ru-mu ga
gozaimasu*

Yes, we have a
double room.

ルームサービス
はありますか？
*ru-mu sahbisu
wa arimasuka*

Is there room service?

4 Words to remember (4 minutes)

Familiarize yourself with these words and test yourself by concealing the Japanese on the right with the cover flap.

部屋から海が見えますか？
heya kara umi ga mie masuka
Does the room have a sea view?

5 Say it (2 minutes)

Do you have any single rooms?

For two nights.

Is dinner included?

room	部屋	*heya*
single room	シングルルーム	*shinguru ru-mu*
double room	ダブルルーム	*daburu ru-mu*
twin room	ツインルーム	*tsuin ru-mu*
bathroom	バス	*basu*
shower	シャワー	*shawah*
breakfast	朝食	*chohshoku*
key	キー	*kih*
balcony	バルコニー	*barukonih*
two nights	二泊	*ni haku*
three nights	三泊	*san paku*

Cultural tip Japanese hotel rooms tend to include a pair of house slippers as a matter of course. You are assumed to want to remove your shoes in the room, as you would at home. Hotel staff address customers using ultra-polite, uncommon Japanese expressions.

はい。何泊のご予定ですか？
hai. nan paku no goyoteh desuka

Yes. How many nights?

三泊です。
san paku desu

For three nights.

かしこまりました。これがキーです。
kashikomari mashita. kore ga kih desu

Very good. Here's your key.

HOTERU DE
In the hotel

As well as slippers, you will nearly always find a traditional Japanese robe/pyjamas (**yukata**) in your room – usually laid out on the bed. This is the case even in the international chains. Non-smoking rooms are sometimes offered, but exclusively non-smoking floors are not always available.

2 Match and repeat (6 minutes)

Match the numbered items in this hotel bedroom with the Japanese text in the panel and test yourself using the cover flap.

❶ ベッドサイド
テーブル
beddo saido tehburu

❷ ランプ
ranpu

❸ カーテン
kahten

❹ ソファ
sofa

❺ 枕
makura

❻ ベッド
beddo

❼ ベッドスプレッド
beddo supureddo

❽ 毛布
mohfu

❶ bedside table
❷ lamp
curtains ❸
sofa ❹
❻ bed
❽ blanket
❺ pillow
❼ bedspread

Cultural tip Japanese bathrooms can be a culture shock to visitors. The bathtubs are smaller as they are generally only used for soaping yourself before rinsing under the shower. The toilets often feature hi-tech gadgets, such as heated seats. Some even act as automatic bidets, with an in-built washer and drier.

3 Useful phrases (5 minutes)

Learn these phrases and then test yourself using the cover flap.

The room is too hot.　部屋が暑すぎます。
heya ga atsu sugi masu

The room is too cold.　部屋が寒すぎます。
heya ga samu sugi masu

There aren't any towels.　タオルが
ありません。
taoru ga arimasen

I'd like some soap.　石けんを下さい。
sekken o kudasai

The shower seems to be broken.　シャワーが壊れて
いるようです。
shawah ga kowarete iruyoh desu

4 Put into practice (3 minutes)

Cover the text on the right and then complete the dialogue in Japanese.

はい、フロントで
ございます。
hai, furonto de gozaimasu

Yes, front desk.

Say: Are there any pillows?

枕はありますか？
makura wa arimasuka

部屋の担当者が
持って参ります。
heya no tantoh-sha ga motte mairimasu

The staff will bring you some.

Say: And the television seems to be broken.

それからテレビが壊れて
いるようです。
sorekara terebi ga kowarete iruyoh desu

RYOKAN TO ONSEN
Inns and spas

What is Japanese for "shower" (pp.60-1), and "swimming pool"? (pp.48-9)

Say "I'd like some towels". (pp.60-1)

Traditional Japanese *inns*, **ryokan**, and *spas with hot springs*, **onsen**, are often based in beautiful surroundings and offer a haven of peace. Prices are usually inclusive of accommodation and all meals. Additional health treatments such as massage are often also available.

2 Match and repeat (4 minutes)

Learn these phrases and then test yourself by concealing the Japanese with the cover flap.

❶ ふすま
fusuma

❷ 浴衣
yukata

❸ 鏡台
kyodai

❹ 障子
shoji

❺ 畳
tatami

❻ 布団
futon

❷ pyjamas

vanity box ❸

screen ❶ door

futon ❻

3 In conversation: (5 minutes)

二泊したいのですが。
ni haku shitai no desuga

I'd like to stay for two nights.

かしこまりました。
kashikomari mashita

Certainly.

この旅館に温泉は
ありますか？
kono ryokan ni onsen wa arimasuka

Is there a hot spring (tub) in the inn?

4 Say it (2 minutes)

I'd like to stay for five nights.

Is there a swimming pool in the inn?

Can I rent *yukata* pyjamas?

4 screen window

5 tatami mat

5 Useful phrases (3 minutes)

Learn these phrases. Read the English under the pictures and say the phrase in Japanese as shown on the right. Then cover up the answers on the right and test yourself.

どんなタイプの温泉
ですか？
*donna taipu no
onsen desuka*

What type of hot springs do you have?

サウナはありますか？
sauna wa arimasuka

Is there a sauna?

マッサージを予約
できますか？
*massahji o yoyaku
dekimasuka*

Can I book a massage?

タオルを借りることが
できますか？
*taoru o karirukoto
ga dekimasuka*

Can I rent a towel?

はい。屋上に
ございます。
*hai. okujoh ni
gozaimasu*

Yes, it's located on the roof.

タオルを借りることが
できますか？
*taoru o karirukoto ga
dekimasuka*

Can I rent a towel?

入り口で貸し出して
おります。
*iriguchi de kashidashite
orimasu*

You can rent one at the spa entrance.

1 **Warm up** (1 minute)

How do you say
"My son has a car"?
(pp.14-15)

What is the Japanese
for "room", "bed", and
"pillow"? (pp.60-1)

KEIYOH-SHI
Adjectives

Basic adjectives (descriptive words) are quite simple to use in Japanese: car(s) is **kuruma**; small car(s) is **chihsai kuruma**. In a sentence, the word order is: item(s) + **wa/ ga** (as for) + adjective + **desu**, for example **kuruma wa chihsai desu** (The car is small); **yama wa takai desu** (The mountains are high).

2 **Words to remember** (7 minutes)

There are no plurals in Japanese. So *the mountain is high* and *the mountains are high* would both be **yama wa takai desu**.

大きい ohkih	big, large
小さい chihsai	small
高い takai	high, tall
低い hikui	short
暑い atsui	hot
冷たい tsumetai	cold
静か shizuka	quiet
うるさい urusai	noisy
硬い katai	hard
柔らかい yawarakai	soft
美しい utsukushih	beautiful

山は高いです。
yama wa takai desu
The mountains
are high.

森が綺麗です。
mori ga kireh desu
The forest is
beautiful.

Read it All of the adjectives above except *noisy* are written in a mixture of *kanji* and *hiragana* characters. The first *kanji* character carries the core meaning, for example 大 (*big*), 美 (*beautiful*). The attached *hiragana* characters are grammatical endings. Look up the *hiragana* characters in the table on pp.158-9 to identify the syllables they represent.

寺は古いです。
tera wa furui desu
The temple is old.

あの橋はとても狭いです。
ano hashi wa totemo semai desu
That bridge is very narrow.

3 Useful phrases (4 minutes)

You can emphasize a description by using *totemo* (very) before the adjective: *totemo urusai* (very noisy).

The coffee is cold.	コーヒーが冷たいです。 *koh-hi ga tsumetai desu*
My room is very noisy.	私の部屋はとてもうるさいです。 *watashi no heya wa totemo urusai desu*
This car is very small.	この車はとても小さいです。 *kono kuruma wa totemo chihsai desu*
This bed is hard.	このベッドは硬いです。 *kono beddo wa katai desu*

4 Put into practice (3 minutes)

Join in this conversation. Cover up the text on the right and complete the dialogue in Japanese. Check and repeat if necessary.

こちらが部屋です。
kochira ga heya desu
Here's the room.

Say: The view is very beautiful.

景色がとても美しいです。
keshiki ga totemo utsukushih desu

バスルームはあちらです。
basu ru-mu wa achira desu
The bathroom is over there.

Say: It's very small.

とても小さいです。
totemo chihsai desu

あいにく他には部屋はございません。
ainiku hoka niwa heya wa gozaimasen
Unfortunately, there aren't any other rooms.

Say: We'll take it.

これにします。
kore ni shimasu

Kotae
Answers (Cover with flap)

FUKUSHU TO KURIKAESHI
Review and repeat

1 Adjectives

❶ 大きい
ohkih

❷ 柔らかい
yawarakai

❸ 古い
furui

❹ 静か
shizuka

❺ 冷たい
tsumetai

1 Adjectives (3 minutes)

Put the word in brackets into Japanese.

❶ *ie wa* _____ *desu.* (big)

❷ *beddo wa* _____ *desu.* (soft)

❸ *tera wa totemo* _____ *desu.* (old)

❹ *watashi no heya wa* _____ *desu.* (quiet)

❺ *mizu ga totemo* _____ *desu.* (cold)

2 Inns

❶ ふすま
fusuma

❷ 浴衣
yukata

❸ 鏡台
kyodai

❹ 布団
futon

❺ 障子
shoji

❻ 畳
tatami

2 Inns (3 minutes)

Name these items you might find in a traditional Japanese inn.

❶ screen door
❷ pyjamas
❸ vanity box
❹ futon
❺ screen window

Kotae
Answers (Cover with flap)

3 At the hotel (4 minutes)

You are booking a room in a hotel. Follow the conversation, replying in Japanese using the English prompts.

hai, dohzo
❶ Do you have any rooms?

hai. nanpaku no goyoteh desuka
❷ Five nights.

kashikomari mashita
❸ Is breakfast included?

ihe. go-hyaku yen desu
❹ We'll take it.

3 At the hotel

❶ 空いている部屋は
ありますか?
*aiteiru heya wa
arimasuka*

❷ 五泊です。
go haku desu

❸ 朝食込みですか?
*chohshoku komi
desuka*

❹ これにします。
kore ni shimasu

4 Negatives (5 minutes)

Make these sentences negative using *wa arimasen*.

❶ *taoru wa arimasu*

❷ *ru-mu sahbisu wa arimasu*

❸ *kono ryokan ni onsen
wa arimasu*

❹ *kono machi ni hakubutsu
kan wa arimasu*

❺ *meishi wa arimasu*

tatami mat ❻

4 Negatives

❶ タオルは
ありません。
taoru wa arimasen

❷ ルームサービス
はありません。
*ru-mu sahbisu wa
arimasen*

❸ この旅館に温泉は
ありません。
*kono ryokan ni onsen
wa arimasen*

❹ この街に博物館はあ
りません。
*kono machi ni
hakubutsu kan wa
arimasen*

❺ 名刺はありません。
meishi wa arimasen

1 Warm up (1 minute)

Ask "Can I use a credit card?" (p.39)

Say "Turn left at the traffic lights", and "The station is near the café". (pp.50-1)

DEPAHTO
Department store

In recent years, many Japanese have started buying food and other provisions in **depahto**. The basement floor of department stores usually houses a food "market" with separate stalls. However, many towns also have shopping arcades, often adjacent to local train stations.

2 Match and repeat (5 minutes)

Notice the Japanese word *ya*, meaning *shop*: *pan ya*, *bread shop* (baker); *niku ya*, *meat shop* (butcher), etc. Match the shops numbered 1-9 on the right to the Japanese in the panel.

❶ パン屋
pan ya

❷ ケーキ屋
kehki ya

❸ 酒屋
saka ya

❹ デリカテッセン
derikatessen

❺ 八百屋
yao ya

❻ 本屋
hon ya

❼ 魚屋
sakana ya

❽ 肉屋
niku ya

❾ 豆腐屋
tofu ya

❶ baker

❷ cake shop

❹ delicatessen

❺ greengrocer

❼ fishmonger

❽ butcher

Cultural tip Department stores will often have a folk art section (*kyohdo zaiku*). Here you can buy traditional souvenirs such as painted wooden dolls, lanterns, fans, kimonos, parasols, screens, and origami kits. You can also find the famous Japanese **nurimono** (lacquer ware) in the form of decorated bowls, boxes, and pots with natural designs (flowers, birds, etc.). All of these make very good gifts.

花屋はどこですか？
hana ya wa doko desuka
Where's the florist?

❸ off-licence

❻ bookshop

❾ tofu shop

3 Words to remember (4 minutes)

Familiarize yourself with these words and then test yourself.

dairy	乳製品	*nyu seihin*
antique shop	骨董品店	*kotto hin ten*
hairdresser	美容院	*biyoh in*
barber	理容院	*riyoh in*
jeweller	宝石商	*hohseki shoh*
post office	郵便局	*yu-bin kyoku*
florist	花屋	*hana ya*
shoe shop	靴屋	*kutsu ya*
travel agent	旅行代理店	*ryokoh dairi den*

4 Useful phrases (3 minutes)

Familiarize yourself with these phrases.

Where's the hairdresser?	美容院はどこですか？	*biyoh in wa doko desuka*
Where can I pay?	どこで払えますか？	*doko de harae masuka*
I'm just looking. Thanks.	見ているだけです。どうも。	*mite iru dake desu. dohmo*
Do you have phonecards? ("Are there phonecards?")	テレカはありますか？	*tereka wa arimasuka*
Can I exchange this?	交換できますか？	*kohkan dekimasuka*
Can you give me the receipt?	レシートをもらえますか？	*reshihto o morae masuka*
I'd like to place an order for...	...を注文したいです。	*...o chu-mon shitai desu*

5 Say it (2 minutes)

Where's the baker?

Do you have towels?

I'd like to place an order for curtains.

1 Warm up (1 minute)

What are "forty", "seventy", "a hundred", "a thousand", and "ten thousand" in Japanese? (pp.30-1)

Say "big" and "small" in Japanese. (pp.64-5)

DENKIYA
Electronics store

Tokyo is home to probably the world's largest concentration of electronics stores in the famous Akihabara "electric town". Here you can find a huge range of computers, cameras, gadgets, and parts, both new and second-hand. Guarantees vary, and you need to check the equipment will work at home.

2 Match and repeat (4 minutes)

Match the numbered items to the Japanese words in the panel below and test yourself using the cover flap.

❶ マウス
   mausu

❷ アダプタ
   adaputa

❸ トランスフォーマー
   toransufomar

❹ パソコン
   pasokon

❺ 画面
   gamen

❻ 保証書
   hoshoh-sho

❼ メモリー
   memori

❽ バッテリー
   batteri

Read it When you see price labels, you will usually see the symbol for **yen** (¥), or sometimes the character 円, with the price in Western figures. The full-stop and dash after the amount mean *and no more*.

❶ mouse
transformer ❸
adapter ❷
memory ❼
❽ battery
guarantee ❻

3 In conversation (5 minutes)

あのパソコンは
いくらですか？
ano pasokon wa ikura desuka

How much is that laptop computer?

税込み10万円です。
zeikomi jyu-man yen desu

It's 100,000 yen including tax.

ハードディスクの
容量はいくらですか？
hardo disuku no yoryo wa ikura desuka

How big is the hard disk?

Cultural tip The Japanese currency system is the **yen** (¥). As each yen is worth less than 1p, you'll generally be spending thousands, or even tens of thousands of them. Banknote denominations go up to ¥10,000, so be careful not to confuse the number of zeros.

❹ laptop

❺ screen

4 Useful phrases (5 minutes)

Learn these phrases. Then conceal the answers on the right using the cover flap. Read the English under the pictures and say the phrase in Japanese as shown on the right.

That camera is too expensive.

あのカメラは
高すぎます。
*ano kamera wa
takasugi masu*

How much is that one?

あれはいくら
ですか？
a-re wa ikura desuka

Will it work in England?

イギリスで
使えますか？
igirisu de tsukae masuka

40ギガで、メモリーは1ギガ
です。
*yonjyu giga de memori wa
ichi giga desu*

40 gigabytes, and one
gigabyte of memory.

イギリスで使え
ますか？
igirisu de tsukae masuka

Will it work in England?

はい。ただしトランスフォー
マーが必要です。
*hai. tadashi toransufomar
ga hitsuyo desu*

Yes, but you need
a transformer.

SU-PAH DE
At the supermarket

Japanese supermarkets are often more like hypermarkets, selling household items and clothes as well as food and essentials. Most Japanese still pay for their groceries in cash. Paying by card at a supermarket is still not common, but cards are frequently used in other stores, such as clothing stores.

1 Warm up (1 minute)

What are these items, which you could buy in a supermarket? (pp.22-3)

yasai
kudamono
shifudo
kome
wain
mizu

2 Match and repeat (5 minutes)

Look at the numbered items and match them to the Japanese words in the panel below.

❶ 家庭用品
kateh yo-hin

❷ 果物
kudamono

❸ 飲み物
nomimono

❹ 加工食品
kakoh shokuhin

❺ 野菜
yasai

❻ 冷凍食品
reitoh shokuhin

❼ 菓子類
kashi rui

❽ 化粧品
keshoh hin

household products ❶

fruit ❷

drinks ❸

ready ❹
meals

vegetables ❺

frozen foods ❻

Cultural tip Supermarkets usually pre-package fresh produce such as meat, fish, fruit, vegetables, and cheese. You just pick up the pre-priced packet you want and take it to the checkout.

3 Useful phrases (3 minutes)

Learn these phrases and then test yourself using the cover flap.

May I have a bag, please?	ビニール袋をもらえますか？ *binihru bukuro o moraemasuka*
Where's the drinks section?	飲み物類はどこですか？ *nomimono rui wa doko desuka*
Where's the checkout?	レジはどこですか？ *reji wa doko desuka*
Where are the shopping trolleys?	ショッピングカートはどこですか？ *shoppingu kahto wa doko desuka*

4 Words to remember (4 minutes)

8 beauty products

7 snacks

Learn these words and then test yourself using the cover flap.

bread	パン *pan*
milk	牛乳 *gyu-nyu*
butter	バター *batah*
dairy products	乳製品 *nyu seihin*
ham	ハム *hamu*
salt	塩 *shio*
pepper	胡椒 *koshoh*
toilet paper	トイレットペーパー *toiretto pehpah*
nappies	オムツ *omutsu*
washing-up liquid	食器用洗剤 *shokki yoh senzai*

5 Say it (2 minutes)

Where's the toilet paper?

May I have some butter, please?

Is there any ham?

FUKU TO KUTSU
Clothes and shoes

Loan words are used for most Western-style clothes: *pantsu* (*trousers*), *jyaketto* (*jacket*), etc. Only items that existed traditionally have Japanese names: *kutsu* (*shoes*), *sode* (*sleeves*). Other traditional articles, such as the *kimono*, *obi* (*sash*), and *geta* (*clogs*) are now largely reserved for special occasions.

1   Warm up (1 minute)

Say "A..., please". (pp.24-5)

Ask "Is there a...?" (pp.48-9)

Say "thirteen", "twenty-four", and "thirty" in Japanese. (pp.30-1)

Say "big" and "small" in Japanese. (pp.64-5)

2   Match and repeat (4 minutes)

Match the numbered items of clothing to the Japanese words in the panel below. Test yourself using the cover flap.

❶ シャツ
  shatsu

❷ ネクタイ
  nekutai

❸ 袖
  sode

❹ ジャケット
  jyaketto

❺ ポケット
  poketto

❻ パンツ
  pantsu

❼ スカート
  sukahto

❽ ストッキング
  sutokkingu

❾ 靴
  kutsu

shirt ❶

tie ❷

sleeve ❸

jacket ❹

pocket ❺

trousers ❻

Cultural tip Japan has its own system of sizes. Generally, for women's clothes add two to get Japanese sizes. For example, British size 10 is Japanese 12, British 12 is Japanese 14. A Japanese shoe size 23 is roughly equivalent to a size 4, 24 is a size 5, and so on. Even allowing for conversion of sizes, Japanese clothes tend to be cut very small.

3 Useful phrases (5 minutes)

Learn these phrases and then test yourself using the cover flap.

Do you have a larger size?	もっと大きいサイズがありますか？ *motto ohkih saizu ga arimasuka*
It's not what I want.	わたしが欲しいものではありません。 *watashi ga hoshih mono dewa arimasen*
I'll take the pink one.	ピンクのを買います。 *pinku no o kaimasu*

4 Words to remember (5 minutes)

Colours are adjectives (see p.64). Below you will see the pure form of the colours, but you may find that endings have been added to the word depending on the sentence.

red	赤 *aka*
white	白 *shiro*
blue	青 *ao*
yellow	黄色 *ki iro*
green	緑 *midori*
black	黒 *kuro*

❼ skirt

❽ tights

❾ shoes

Read it All the items of clothing in section 2, except *shoes* and *sleeve*, are written in *katakana*, the script used for foreign loan words. Use the *katakana* table on pp.158-9 to work out the syllables in each word.

Kotae
Answers (Cover with flap)

FUKUSHU TO KURIKAESH
Review and repeat

1 Electronic

❶ マウス
mausu

❷ アダプタ
adaputa

❸ トランスフォーマー
toransufomar

❹ 画面
gamen

❺ バッテリー
batteri

❻ メモリー
memori

❼ 保証書
hoshoh-sho

❽ パソコン
pasokon

1 Electronic (3 minutes)

Name the numbered items in Japanese.

❹ screen
❶ mouse
transformer ❸
adapter ❷
memory ❻
❺ battery
❼ guarantee
❽ laptop

2 Description

❶ That camera is
too expensive.

❷ My room is
very noisy.

❸ Do you have
a larger size?

2 Description (2 minutes)

What do these phrases mean?

❶ *ano kamera wa takasugi masu*

❷ *watashi no heya wa totemo urusai desu*

❸ *motto ohkih saizu ga arimasuka*

3 Shops

❶ パン屋
pan ya

❷ デリカテッセン
derikatessen

❸ 八百屋
yao ya

❹ 魚屋
sakana ya

❺ ケーキ屋
kehki ya

❻ 肉屋
niku ya

3 Shops (3 minutes)

Name the numbered shops in Japanese. Then
check your answers.

❶ baker

❷ delicatessen

❸ greengrocer

❹ fishmonger

❺ cake shop

❻ butcher

Kotae
Answers (Cover with flap)

4 Supermarket (3 minutes)

What is the Japanese for the numbered product categories?

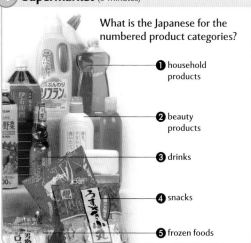

1 household products

2 beauty products

3 drinks

4 snacks

5 frozen foods

4 Supermarket

1 家庭用品
kateh yo-hin

2 化粧品
keshoh hin

3 飲み物
nomimono

4 菓子類
kashi rui

5 冷凍食品
reitoh shokuhin

5 Museum (4 minutes)

Join in this conversation replying in Japanese following the English prompts.

hai, dohzo
1 I'd like four tickets.

happyaku yen ni narimasu
2 What time do you close?

roku ji ni shimari masu
3 Is there a guidebook?

dohzo. gaido bukku wa muryoh desu
4 Where's the lift?

achira ni erebehtah ga arimasu
5 Thank you very much.

5 Museum

1 チケットを四枚お願いします。
chiketto o yonmai onegai shimasu

2 何時に閉まりますか？
nanji ni shimarimasuka

3 ガイドブックはありますか？
gaido bukku wa arimasuka

4 エレベーターはどこですか？
erebehtah wa doko desuka

5 どうもありがとうございます。
dohmo arigatoh gozaimasu

SHIGOTO
Jobs

1 Warm up (1 minute)

Say "Akiko is a student" and "I'm English".
(pp.14-15)

Say "The internet café is in the centre of town".
(pp.48-9)

Japanese has some generic, non-job specific words used to refer mainly to office workers: the self-explanatory **sararihman** (*salary man*) and the **OL** (pronounced "oh-el" and meaning *office lady*) being two of the most common. **Sengyo-shufu** (literally *specialist*) is used to mean *housewife*.

2 Words to remember: jobs (7 minutes)

Familiarize yourself with these Japanese words and test yourself using the flap.

医者 *isha*	doctor
歯医者 *ha-isha*	dentist
看護師 *kangoshi*	nurse
先生 *sensei*	teacher
会計士 *kaikehshi*	accountant
弁護士 *bengoshi*	lawyer
デザイナー *dezainah*	designer
秘書 *hisho*	secretary
店主 *tenshu*	shopkeeper
電気技師 *denki gishi*	electrician
配管工 *haikankoh*	plumber
コック *kokku*	cook
自営業 *ji-eigyoh*	self-employed
学生 *gakusei*	student

会社員です。
kaisha in desu
I'm a businessman.

会計士です。
kaikehshi desu
I'm an accountant.

3 Put into practice (4 minutes)

Join in this conversation. Use the cover flap to conceal the text on the right and complete the dialogue in Japanese.

ご職業は？ *goshokugyoh wa*	会計士です。 *kaikehshi desu*

What's your profession?

Say: I'm an accountant.

どこの会社にお勤めですか？ *doko no kaisha ni otsutomete desuka*	自営業です。 *ji-eigyoh desu*

What company do you work for?

Say: I'm self-employed.

ああ、そうなんですか！ *ah, sohnandesuka*	ご職業は？ *goshokugyoh wa*

Oh, really!

Ask: What's your profession?

Cultural tip There are different titles for manager depending on the level. The order of seniority is 社長 *shacho* (MD), 専務 *senmu* (division), 部長 *bucho* (department), 課長 *kacho* (section), 係長 *kakaricho* (team). Look out for the titles on business cards.

4 Words to remember: workplace (3 minutes)

本社は大阪にあります。
honsha wa Osaka ni arimasu
The head office is in Osaka.

Familiarize yourself with these words and test yourself.

head office	本社 *honsha*
branch	支店 *shiten*
...department	...部 *...bu*
office worker	会社員 *kaisha in*
manager	マネージャー *manehjyah*

Warm up (1 minute)

Practise different ways
of introducing yourself
in different situations
(pp.8-9). Mention your
name, occupation, and
any other information
you'd like to volunteer
(pp.12-13, pp.14-15).

OFISU
The office

Traditionally most adult Japanese would have an *inkan*,
an official seal or stamp unique to the individual and
used to sign papers and forms. You may still see these
stamps on official government papers and high-level
contracts, although they are no longer the necessity
they once were.

2 **Words to remember** (5 minutes)

Familiarize yourself with these words. Read them aloud several
times and try to memorize them. Conceal the Japanese with
the cover flap and test yourself.

コンピュータ *konpyu-tah*	computer
マウス *mausu*	mouse
メール *mehru*	e-mail
インターネット *intahnetto*	internet
パスワード *pasuwahdo*	password
ボイスメール *boisu mehru*	voicemail
ファックス *fakkusu*	fax machine
コピー *kopih*	photocopy
コピー機 *kopihki*	photocopier ("copy machine")
本 *hon*	book
手帳 *techoh*	diary
名刺 *meishi*	business card
ミーティング *mihtingu*	meeting
コンフェレンス *konferensu*	conference
会議事項 *kaigi jikoh*	agenda

lamp **1**

screen **4**

laptop **6**

keyboard **5**

2 stapler

telephone **3**

drawer **12**

pen **10**　**11** notepad

desk **7**

3 Useful phrases (2 minutes)

Learn these phrases and then test yourself using the cover flap.

I need to make some photocopies.	コピーをとる必要があります。 *kopih o toru hitsuyoh ga arimasu*
I'd like to arrange an appointment.	アポを取りたいのですが。 *apo o toritai no desuga*
I want to send an e-mail.	メールを送りたいです。 *mehru o okuritai desu*

4 Match and repeat (5 minutes)

Match the numbered items to the Japanese words on the right.

clock ⑧

printer ⑨

⑬ swivel chair

❶ ランプ
ranpu

❷ ホチキス
hochikisu

❸ 電話
denwa

❹ 画面
gamen

❺ キーボード
kihbohdo

❻ パソコン
pasokon

❼ 机
tsukue

❽ 時計
tokei

❾ プリンター
purintah

❿ ペン
pen

⓫ ノート
nohto

⓬ 引き出し
hikidashi

⓭ 回転椅子
kaiten isu

5 Say it (2 minutes)

I'd like to arrange a meeting.

I want to send a fax.

Is there an agenda?

GAKKAI DE
At the conference

University courses usually last four years and entrance to the top colleges is very competitive. High schools often start to prepare for the entrance exam many years in advance as future prospects can depend on which university a student attends. Once there, the pressure is less intense.

1 Warm up (1 minute)

Say "Oh, really?" (pp.78-9), "meeting" (pp.80-1), and "appointment". (pp.32-3)

Ask "What's your profession?" and answer "I'm a lawyer". (pp.78-9)

2 Useful phrases (3 minutes)

Learn these phrases and then test yourself using the cover flap.

ご専門は？
gosenmon wa

What's your field?

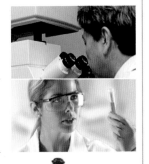

研究をしています。
kenkyu o shiteimasu

I'm doing research.

法律を勉強しました。
hohritsu o benkyoh shimashita

I have a degree in law.

建築学の講師です。
kenchiku gaku no kohshi desu

I'm a lecturer in architecture.

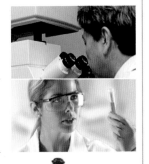

3 In conversation (5 minutes)

こんにちは。岡田
です。
konnichiwa. Okada desu

Hello, I'm Okada.

どこで教えていらっしゃいますか？
doko de oshiete irasshai masuka

Where do you teach?

東京大学です。
Tokyo daigaku desu

I teach at Tokyo University.

4 Words to remember (4 minutes)

Familiarize yourself with these words and then test yourself.

展示会には私達の
スタンドがあります。
*tenji kai niwa watashitachi
no sutando ga arimasu*
There's our exhibition stand.

conference (academic)	学会 *gakkai*
lecture	講義 *kohgi*
seminar	ゼミ *zemi*
lecture theatre	講堂 *kohdoh*
exhibition	展示会 *tenji kai*
university lecturer	大学講師 *daigaku kohshi*
professor	教授 *kyohjyu*
medicine	医学 *igaku*
science	科学 *kagaku*
literature	文学 *bungaku*
engineering	工学 *kohgaku*
law	法律 *hohritsu*
architecture	建築学 *kenchiku gaku*
information technology	IT *"ai-tih"*

5 Say it (2 minutes)

I teach at London University.

I have a degree in medicine.

I'm a lecturer in engineering.

ご専門は？
gosenmon wa

What's your field?

物理です。研究もしています。
butsuri desu. kenkyu mo shiteimasu

Physics. I'm also doing research.

ああ、そうですか？
ah, sohdesuka

Oh, really?

1 Warm up (1 minute)

Say "I want to send an e-mail". (pp.80-1)

Say "I'd like to arrange an appointment". (pp.80-1)

BIJINESU
In business

You will make a good impression if you make the effort to begin a meeting with a few words in Japanese, even if your vocabulary is limited. After that, all parties will probably be happy to continue in English. Remember to take business cards to exchange at meetings.

2 Words to remember (6 minutes)

Familiarize yourself with these words and then test yourself by concealing the Japanese with the cover flap.

注文	order
chu-mon	
配達	delivery
haitatsu	
支払い	payment
shiharai	
予算	budget
yosan	
値段	price
nedan	
証書	documents
shohsho	
請求書	invoice
sehkyu-sho	
見積もり	estimate
mitsumori	
利益	profits
ri-eki	
売り上げ	sales
uri age	
合計額	figures
gohkeh gaku	

顧客
kokyaku
client

報告書
hohkoku sho
report

Cultural tip In general, business dealings are formal. However, the Japanese are famous for their hospitality. Visitors are often escorted from the moment they wake up to the moment they go to bed. It's a good idea to take presents from home to show your appreciation.

契約書を見せてください。
kehyaku sho o misete kudasai
Please show me the contract.

重役
jyu-yaku
executive

3 Useful phrases (6 minutes)

Practise these phrases. Notice that the Japanese is necessarily very polite. It's better to err on the side of caution in a business context.

契約書を送ってください
ますか？
*kehyaku sho o okutte
kudasai masuka*

Can you send me the contract, please?

値段は決まりましたか？
nedan wa kimarimashitaka

Have we agreed a price?

配達はいつになりますか？
*haitatsu wa itsu ni
nari masuka*

When can you make the delivery?

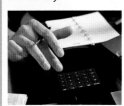

予算はおいくら
ですか？
yosan wa oikura desuka

What's the budget?

Read it Some traditional Japanese words used in a business context have alternative English loan words. These imported words will be written in *katakana* characters. For example, you may see the following alternatives for the traditional words in this lesson. See if you can work out the individual syllables of the words using the *katakana* table on pp.158-9.

オーダー *ohdah* order

ドキュメント *dokyumento* document

レポート *repohto* report

4 Say it (2 minutes)

Can you send me the invoice, please?

What's the price?

Please show me the order.

Kotae
Answers (Cover with flap)

FUKUSHU TO KURIKAESHI
Review and repeat

1 At the office

❶ ランプ
ranpu

❷ パソコン
pasokon

❸ ノート
nohto

❹ ホチキス
hochikisu

❺ 机
tsukue

❻ ペン
pen

❼ 時計
tokei

1 At the office (4 minutes)

Name these items in Japanese.

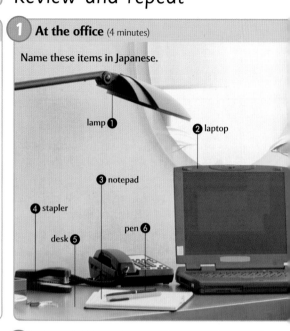

lamp ❶
❷ laptop
❸ notepad
❹ stapler
desk ❺
pen ❻

2 Jobs

❶ 医者
isha

❷ 配管工
haikankoh

❸ 店主
tenshu

❹ 会計士
kaikehshi

❺ 学生
gakusei

❻ 弁護士
bengoshi

2 Jobs (3 minutes)

What are these jobs in Japanese?

❶ doctor

❷ plumber

❸ shopkeeper

❹ accountant

❺ student

❻ lawyer

3 Work (4 minutes)

Answer these questions following the English prompts.

goshokugyoh wa
❶ Say "I'm a dentist".

doko no kaisha ni otsutome desuka
❷ Say "I'm self-employed".

doko de oshiete irasshai masuka
❸ Say "I teach at Tokyo university".

moshi moshi
❹ Say "I'd like to arrange an appointment".

clock ❼

3 Work

❶ 歯医者です。
ha-isha desu

❷ 自営業です。
ji-eigyoh desu

❸ 東京大学です。
Tokyo daigaku desu

❹ アポを取りたいの
ですが。
apo o toritai no desuga

4 How much? (4 minutes)

Answer the question with the price shown in brackets.

❶ *koh-hi wa ikura desuka*
(¥300)

❷ *heya wa ikura desuka*
(¥8,000)

❸ *pasokon wa ikura desuka* (¥100,000)

❹ *chiketto wa ikura desuka* (¥700)

4 How much?

❶ 三百円です。
san byaku yen desu

❷ 八千円です。
hassen yen desu

❸ 十万円です。
jyu-man yen desu

❹ 七百円です。
nana hyaku yen desu

YAKKYOKU DE
At the chemist

Warm up (1 minute)

Say "Can you give me the receipt?" (pp.68-9)

Ask "Do you have any cakes?" (pp.18-19)

To describe an ailment you can use the phrase *...ga shimasu* (*I have...*), for example *zutsu ga shimasu* (*I have a headache*), or you could say *...ga itai desu* (*I have a pain in my...*). Notice that the ailment or part of the body comes first in the sentence.

Match and repeat (3 minutes)

Match the numbered items to the Japanese words in the panel below and test yourself using the cover flap.

❶ 包帯
hohtai

❷ シロップ
shiroppu

❸ 目薬
megusuri

❹ 軟膏
nankoh

❺ 絆創膏
bansohkoh

❻ 注射器
chu-sha ki

❼ 座薬
zayaku

❽ 錠剤
jyohzai

bandage ❶

❷ syrup

❹ ointment

drops ❸

plaster ❺

syringe ❻

In conversation (3 minutes)

こんにちは。
どうしましたか？
konnichiwa.
doh shimashitaka

Hello. What's the matter?

腹痛がします。
fukutsu ga shimasu

I have a stomachache.

下痢気味ですか？
geri gimi desuka

Do you also have diarrhoea?

4 **Words to remember** (2 minutes)

Familiarize yourself with these words and test yourself using the flap.

頭痛がします。
zutsu ga shimasu
I have a headache.

headache	頭痛	*zutsu*
stomachache	腹痛	*fukutsu*
diarrhoea	下痢	*geri*
cold	風邪	*kaze*
cough	せき	*seki*
sunburn	日焼け	*hiyake*
toothache	歯痛	*ha-ita*

5 **Say it** (2 minutes)

I have a toothache.

I have a cough.

Do you have that as an ointment?

7 suppository

8 tablet

6 **Useful phrases** (4 minutes)

Learn these phrases and then test yourself using the cover flap.

I have a pain in my leg.	脚が痛いです。 *ashi ga itai desu*
Do you have that as a syrup?	それのシロップは ありますか？ *sore no shiroppu wa arimasuka*
I'm allergic to penicillin.	ペニシリンに対して アレルギー体質です。 *penishirin ni taishite arerugih taishitsu desu*

いいえ、でも頭痛
がします。
ihe, demo zutsu ga shimasu

No, but I have a headache.

これをお飲み下さい。
kore o onomi kudasai

Take this.

それの錠剤は
ありますか？
sore no jyohzai wa arimasuka

Do you have that as tablets?

KARADA
The body

Say "I have a toothache" and "I have a pain in my leg". (pp.88-9)

Ask politely "What's the matter?" (pp.88-9)

Spoken Japanese uses the same pronunciation for leg and foot: *ashi*. However, the written characters are different. There are two separate words describing the back area: *lower back* is **koshi**; *upper back* is **senaka**. Remember there is no plural, so **meh** is *eye* or *eyes*.

2 **Match and repeat: body** (6 minutes)

Match the numbered parts of the body with the list below. Test yourself by using the cover flap.

1 手
   te

2 頭
   atama

3 肩
   kata

4 肘
   hiji

5 髪
   kami

6 腕
   ude

7 首
   kubi

8 胸
   mune

9 お腹
   onaka

10 脚
   ashi

11 膝
   hiza

12 足
   ashi

hand **1**
head **2**
shoulder **3**
4 elbow
5 hair
6 arm
7 neck
8 chest
9 stomach
10 leg
11 knee
12 foot

3 Match and repeat: face (3 minutes)

eye ❶
❷ eyebrow
❸ nose
❹ ear
❺ mouth

Match the numbered facial features with the list below.

❶ 目
meh

❷ 眉
mayu

❸ 鼻
hana

❹ 耳
mimi

❺ 口
kuchi

4 Useful phrases (3 minutes)

Learn these phrases and then test yourself using the cover flap.

I have a pain in my lower back. 腰が痛いです。
koshi ga itai desu

I have a rash on my arm. 腕がかぶれています。
ude ga kaburete imasu

I don't feel well. 調子が悪いです。
chohshi ga warui desu

5 Put into practice (2 minutes)

Join in this conversation and test yourself using the cover flap.

どうしました？ 調子が悪いです。
doh shimashita *chohshi ga warui desu*

What's the matter?

Say: I don't feel well.

どこが痛みますか？ 肩が痛いです。
doko ga itami masuka *kata ga itai desu*

Where does it hurt?

Say: I have a pain in my shoulder.

ISHA TO
With the doctor

1 **Warm up** (1 minute)

Say "I have a headache".
(pp.88-9)

Now, say "I have a pain
in my ear". (pp.90-1)

Ask "What's the matter?"
(pp.88-9)

Most Japanese doctors are based in hospitals rather
than in separate clinics. You will usually need to go
to a hospital for an appointment, even for minor
ailments. Many Japanese doctors speak good English,
but you could need to give a basic explanation in
Japanese, for example, to a receptionist.

2 **Useful phrases you may hear** (3 minutes)

Learn these phrases and then test yourself
using the cover flap to conceal the Japanese
on the left.

大したことはありません。 *taishitakoto wa arimasen*	It's not serious.
検査が必要です。 *kensa ga hitsuyoh desu*	Tests are needed.
骨折です。 *kossetsu desu*	You have a fracture.
入院が必要です。 *nyu-in ga hitsuyoh desu*	You need to stay in hospital. (Literally: hospital is needed.)

今飲んでいる薬は
ありますか？
*ima nondeiru kusuri
wa arimasuka*
Are you taking any medication?

3 **In conversation** (5 minutes)

どうしましたか？
doh shimashitaka

What's the matter?

胸が痛いです。
mune ga itai desu

I have a pain in my chest.

診察しましょう。
shinsatsu shimashoh

I'll need to examine you.

4 Useful phrases you may need to say (4 minutes)

Learn these phrases and then test yourself using the cover flap.

I'm diabetic.	糖尿病です。 *tohnyoh byoh desu*
I'm epileptic.	てんかん持ちです。 *tenkan mochi desu*
I'm asthmatic.	ぜんそく持ちです。 *zensoku mochi desu*
I have a heart condition.	心臓が弱いです。 *shinzoh ga yowai desu*
I have a fever.	熱があります。 *netsu ga arimasu*
It's urgent.	緊急です。 *kinkyu desu*
I feel breathless.	息が苦しいです。 *iki ga kurushih desu*

妊娠しています。
ninshin shite imasu
I'm pregnant.

Cultural tip
There are two separate emergency numbers in Japan depending on which service you require. For the police dial 110, for ambulance and fire service dial 119.

5 Say it (2 minutes)

I have a pain in my arm.

Is it urgent?

重い病気ですか？
omoi byohki desuka

Is it serious?

いいえ、ただの消化不良です。
ihe, tadano shohka furyoh desu

No, you only have indigestion.

よかった！安心しました。
yokatta. anshin shimashita

Good! What a relief.

1 Warm up (1 minute)

Say "Where's the florist?"
(pp.68-9)

Say "Tests are needed".
(pp.92-3)

What is the Japanese for
"mouth" and "head"?
(pp.90-1)

BYOH-IN DE
In hospital

It is useful to know a few basic Japanese phrases
relating to hospitals for use in an emergency or
in case you need to visit a friend or colleague in
hospital. Japanese medical care is excellent but very
expensive, so make sure you have adequate insurance.

2 Useful phrases (5 minutes)

Familiarize yourself with these phrases. Conceal
the Japanese with the cover flap and test yourself.

待合室はどこ ですか？ *machiai shitsu wa doko desuka*	Where's the waiting room?
どのくらいかかり ますか？ *dono kurai kakari masuka*	How long does it take?
痛いですか？ *itai desuka*	Will it hurt?
ベッドに横になって ください。 *beddo ni yoko ni natte kudasai*	Please lie down on the bed.
六時間何も食べないで ください。 *roku jikan nanimo tabenaide kudasai*	Please do not eat anything for six hours.
頭を動かさないで ください。 *atama o ugokasanai de kudasai*	Don't move your head.
口を開けて ください。 *kuchi o akete kudasai*	Open your mouth.
血液検査が必要 です。 *ketsueki kensa ga hitsuyoh desu*	A blood test is needed.

看護師
kangoshi
nurse

具合はいいですか？
guai wa iidesuka
Are you feeling better?

訪問時間はいつですか？
hohmon jikan wa itsu desuka
What are the visiting hours?

3 Words to remember (4 minutes)

レントゲンは正常です。
rentogen wa seijyoh desu
The x-ray is normal.

Memorize these words and test yourself using the cover flap.

emergency ward	緊急病棟 *kinkyu byohtoh*
children's ward	小児病棟 *shohni byohtoh*
operating theatre	手術室 *shujyutsu shitsu*
waiting room	待合室 *machiai shitsu*
corridor	廊下 *rohka*
stairs	階段 *kaidan*
lift	エレベーター *erebehtah*

4 Put into practice (3 minutes)

Join in this conversation. Read the Japanese on the left and follow the instructions to make your reply. Then test yourself by hiding the answers with the cover flap.

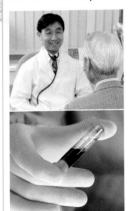

大したことは
ありません。
taishitakoto wa arimasen

It's not serious.

Ask: Are tests needed?

検査が必要ですか？
kensa ga hitsuyoh desuka

血液検査が必要
です。
*ketsueki kensa ga
hitsuyoh desu*

A blood test is needed.

Ask: Will it hurt?

痛いですか？
itai desuka

5 Say it (2 minutes)

Is a blood test needed?

Where's the children's ward?

An x-ray is needed.

Read it It's useful to be able to recognize the Japanese for *hospital*. This literally means *sick building*. The first character 病 **byoh** can also be found in other words such as 病気 **byoh-ki**, *sickness*, and 病人 **byoh-nin**, *sick person*, or *patient*.

病院 **byoh-in** *hospital*

FUKUSHU TO KURIKAESHI
Review and repeat

1 The body

❶ 頭
atama

❷ 腕
ude

❸ 胸
mune

❹ お腹
onaka

❺ 脚
ashi

❻ 膝
hiza

❼ 足
ashi

1 The body (4 minutes)

Name the numbered body parts in Japanese.

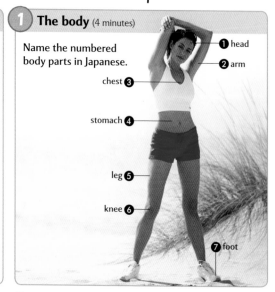

❶ head
❷ arm
chest ❸
stomach ❹
leg ❺
knee ❻
❼ foot

2 On the phone

❶ 大和さんお願いします。
Yamato-san onegai shimasu

❷ ゴープレス・プリンターのジャック・ハントと申します。
Gopress purintah no Jack Hunt to mohshimasu

❸ メッセージを伝えていただけますか？
messehji o tsutaete itadake masuka

❹ ミーティングは火曜日ではありません。
mihtingu wa kayoh bi dewa arimasen

❺ ありがとうございます。
arigatoh gozaimasu

2 On the phone (4 minutes)

You are arranging an appointment. Follow the conversation, replying in Japanese with the help of the numbered English prompts.

moshi moshi, japanihzu konekushon desu
❶ I'd like to speak to Mr Yamato.

dochira sama desuka
❷ Jack Hunt of Gopress Printers.

sumimasenga, ima hanashichu desu
❸ Can I leave a message?

mochiron desu
❹ The meeting isn't on Tuesday.

wakarimashita
❺ Thank you very much.

3 Clothing (3 minutes)

Say the Japanese words for the numbered items of clothing.

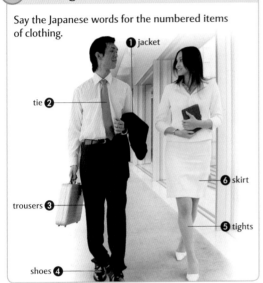

❶ jacket

tie **❷**

trousers **❸**

shoes **❹**

❻ skirt

❺ tights

3 Clothing

❶ ジャケット
jyaketto

❷ ネクタイ
nekutai

❸ パンツ
pantsu

❹ 靴
kutsu

❺ ストッキング
sutokkingu

❻ スカート
sukahto

4 At the doctor's (4 minutes)

Say these phrases in Japanese.

❶ I have a pain in my leg.

❷ Is it serious?

❸ I have a heart condition.

❹ Will it hurt?

❺ I'm pregnant.

4 At the doctor's

❶ 脚が痛いです。
ashi ga itai desu

❷ 重い病気ですか？
omoi byohki desuka

❸ 心臓が弱いです。
shinzoh ga yowai desu

❹ 痛いですか？
itai desuka

❺ 妊娠しています。
ninshin shite imasu

1 Warm up (1 minute)

Say the months of the year in Japanese. (pp.28-9)

Ask "Is there a museum in town?" (pp.48-9) and "How much is that?" (pp.18-19)

IE
Home

In Japan, space is limited and most city-dwellers live in *apartments* (**aparto** or the more luxurious **manshon**). Rooms are often small and a *combined kitchen and dining room* (**dainingu kitchin**) is common. Earthquakes are frequent and buildings have to comply with strict specifications.

2 Match and repeat (5 minutes)

Match the numbered items to the list and test yourself using the flap.

❶ 雨どい
amadoi

❷ バルコニー
barukonih

❸ 窓
mado

❹ 雨戸
amado

❺ 屋根
yane

❻ 壁
kabe

❼ ドア
doa

❽ 階段
kaidan

❾ 庭
niwa

❶ gutter

❷ balcony

❸ window

shutter ❹

garden ❾

steps ❽   door ❼

Cultural tip In addition to being built to withstand earthquakes, most Japanese buildings have steel or wooden anti-typhoon shutters. These can be closed quickly to seal off the house or apartment from raging winds and rain. The hurricane and typhoon season lasts from late August to early October, although storms can occur outside these months.

3 Words to remember (4 minutes)

家賃は一月いくら
ですか？
yachin wa hitotsuki ikura desuka
How much is the rent per month?

 5 roof

Familiarize yourself with these words and
test yourself using the flap.

room	部屋	*heya*
floor	床	*yuka*
ceiling	天井	*ten-jyoh*
bedroom	寝室	*shinshitsu*
bathroom	バスルーム	*basu ru-mu*
kitchen	台所	*daidokoro*
dining room	ダイニングルーム	*dainingu ru-mu*
living room	居間	*ima*
attic	屋根裏	*yane ura*
parking space	車庫	*shako*

wall **6**

4 Useful phrases (3 minutes)

Learn these phrases and test yourself.

車庫はありますか？
shako wa arimasuka

Is there a parking space?

いつ入居できますか？
itsu nyu-kyo dekimasuka

When can I move in?

家具付きですか？
kagu tsuki desuka

Is it furnished?

5 Say it (2 minutes)

Is there a dining room?

Where's the attic?

It's furnished.

1 Warm up (1 minute)

What's the Japanese for "table" (pp.20-1), "desk" (pp.80-1), "bed" (pp.60-1), and "curtains" (pp.60-1)?

How do you say "This car is small"? (pp.64-5)

IE NO NAKA DE
Inside the home

The Japanese often end their sentences with short "markers" that don't really change the meaning but carry different nuances. For example, the **yo** marker can imply *and even* or *to be sure* and **ne** can mean something like *isn't that so?* You'll see examples of these in the conversation below.

2 Match and repeat (3 minutes)

Match the numbered items to the list in the panel below. Then test yourself by concealing the Japanese with the cover flap.

❶ 流し
nagashi

❷ 蛇口
jyaguchi

❸ 炊飯器
sui-hanki

❹ 調理台
chohridai

❺ 食器洗い機
shokki araiki

❻ 椅子
isu

❼ 戸棚
todana

❽ テーブル
tehburu

tap ❷

❶ sink

rice cooker ❸

❺ dishwasher　　chair ❻　　❼ cabinet　　table ❽

3 In conversation (3 minutes)

これが冷蔵庫です。
kore ga reizohko desu

This is the fridge.

炊飯器はありますか？
sui-hanki wa arimasuka

Is there a rice cooker?

はい、そしてこれが
レンジです。
hai, soshite kore ga renji desu

Yes, and here's the stove.

4 Words to remember (2 minutes)

Familiarize yourself with these words
and test yourself using the flap.

このソファは新しいです。
kono sofa wa atarashih desu
This sofa is new.

sofa	ソファ *sofa*
carpet	絨毯 *jyu-tan*
bath	バス *basu*
toilet	トイレ *to-ee-reh*
stove	レンジ *renji*
washing machine	洗濯機 *sentaku ki*
fridge	冷蔵庫 *reizohko*

4 worktop

5 Useful phrases (4 minutes)

Learn these phrases and then test yourself using
the cover flap to conceal the Japanese.

The fridge is broken.	冷蔵庫が壊れて います。 *reizohko ga kowarete imasu*
I'm not fond of the curtains.	カーテンが気に 入りません。 *kahten ga kini irimasen*
Are heat and electricity included?	光熱費込みですか？ *kohnetsu hi komi desuka*

6 Say it (2 minutes)

Is there a washing machine?

The fridge is new.

The tap is broken.

流しが新しいですね。
nagashi ga atarashih desune

The sink is new.

それから食器洗い機
もありますよ。
sorekara shokki araiki mo arimasuyo

And there's even
a dishwasher.

なんてきれいなタイル
なんでしょう！
nante kireh na tairu nandeshoh

What pretty tiles!

NIWA
The garden

1 Warm up (1 minute)

What's the Japanese for "day" and "month"? (pp.28-9)

Say "Where's the florist?" (pp.68-9) and "Is there a garden?" (pp.98-9)

Japanese gardens, often with water features and plants like lilies and cherry trees, can be seen in public places such as parks, temples, and hotels. Space constraints mean that many Japanese homes don't have their own gardens, but house plants and flower arrangements are popular.

2 Words to remember (3 minutes)

Familiarize yourself with these words and test yourself using the flap.

冬 *fuyu*	winter	
春 *haru*	spring	
夏 *natsu*	summer	
秋 *aki*	autumn	

❷ tree

plants ❸

waterfall ❶

flowers ❿

stones ❾

rocks ❽

3 Useful phrases (4 minutes)

Learn these phrases and then test yourself using the cover flap.

What kind of tree is this?	これは何の木 ですか？ *kore wa nanno ki desuka*
I like the pond.	池が好きです。 *ike ga suki desu*
What beautiful flowers!	きれいな花ですね！ *kireh na hana desune*
Can we walk in the garden?	庭を歩いて いいですか？ *niwa o aruite ihdesuka*

4 Match and repeat (5 minutes)

soil **4**

5 path

6 grass

7 pond

Match the numbered items to the words in the panel below.

1 滝
taki

2 木
ki

3 植物
shokubutsu

4 土
tsuchi

5 小道
komichi

6 草
kusa

7 池
ike

8 岩
iwa

9 石
ishi

10 花
hana

5 Say it (2 minutes)

What kind of flower is this?

I like the waterfall.

Is there a pond?

DOHBUTSU
Animals

1 Warm up (1 minute)

Say "My name is John".
(pp.8-9)

Say "I like the pond".
(pp.102-3)

What's "fish" in Japanese?
(pp.22-3)

The Japanese tend to keep small lap dogs and sometimes cats in the house as pets. There is not usually enough space indoors for larger animals. Reptiles and insects, such as snakes and crickets, are also popular, particularly amongst young boys.

2 Match and repeat (3 minutes)

Match the numbered animals to the Japanese words in the panel below. Then test yourself using the cover flap.

❶ 猫
neko

❷ 鳥
tori

❸ 魚
sakana

❹ 犬
inu

❺ 馬
uma

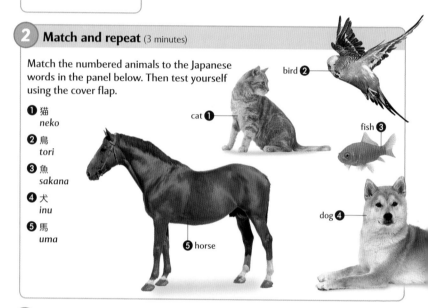

bird ❷

cat ❶

fish ❸

dog ❹

❺ horse

3 Useful phrases (4 minutes)

Learn these phrases and then test yourself using the cover flap.

この犬はおとなしいですか？ *kono inu wa otonashih desuka*	Is this dog friendly?
名前は何ですか？ *namae wa nandesuka*	What's his name?
猫は苦手です。 *neko wa negate desu*	I'm not keen on cats.
この犬は噛みつきませんよ。 *kono inu wa kamitsuki masenyo*	This dog doesn't bite.

あなたの猫ですか？
anata no neko desuka
Is this your cat?

猛犬に注意
Beware of the Dog

Cultural tip Some buildings will keep larger dogs outside as guard dogs. Native Japanese dog breeds, such as the Kishuken, Shibaken, and Ainuken, are known for their toughness and are employed as "yard" dogs rather than treated as pets.

あれは何という魚
ですか？
a-re wa nanto yu sakana desuka
What's that fish called?

4 Words to remember (4 minutes)

Familiarize yourself with these words and test yourself using the flap.

monkey	猿	*saru*
sheep	羊	*hitsuji*
cow	牛	*ushi*
pig	豚	*buta*
rabbit	兎	*usagi*
mouse	ネズミ	*nezumi*

Read it Most basic words referring to natural features or animals, such as *tree*, *dog*, *flower*, *cow*, etc., are written in *kanji* - often with just a single character. Look at the *kanji* for animals on this page and see if you can spot them in the example phrases.

5 Put into practice (3 minutes)

Join in this conversation. Read the Japanese on the left and follow the instructions to make your reply. Then test yourself by concealing the answers with the cover flap.

あなたの犬ですか？
anata no inu desuka

Is this your dog?

Say: Yes, his name is Ichiroh.

はい、イチローと
いいます。
hai, Ichiroh to ihmasu

犬は苦手です。
inu wa negate desu

I'm not keen on dogs.

Say: Don't worry. He's friendly.

大丈夫です。
おとなしいですよ。
daijyohbu desu. otonashih desu yo.

Kotae
Answers (Cover with flap)

FUKUSHU TO KURIKAESHI
Review and repeat

1 Colours

❶ 白
shiro

❷ 黄色
ki iro

❸ 緑
midori

❹ 黒
kuro

❺ 赤
aka

❻ 青
ao

❼ ピンク
pinku

1 Colours (4 minutes)

What are these colours in Japanese?

❶ white
❷ yellow
❸ green
❹ black
❺ red
❻ blue
❼ pink

2 Kitchen

❶ 調理台
chohridai

❷ 流し
nagashi

❸ 蛇口
jyaguchi

❹ 炊飯器
sui-hanki

❺ 食器洗い機
shokki araiki

❻ 椅子
isu

❼ 戸棚
todana

❽ テーブル
tehburu

2 Kitchen (4 minutes)

Say the Japanese words for the numbered items.

worktop ❶   sink ❷   ❸ tap

rice ❹ cooker

dishwasher ❺   chair ❻   cabinet ❼

3 House (4 minutes)

You are visiting a house in Japan. Join in the conversation, replying in Japanese where you see the numbered English prompts.

basu ru-mu wa kochira desu
❶ What pretty tiles!

daidokoro wa ohkih desu
❷ Is there a washing machine?

hai, sorekara shokki araiki mo arimasuyo
❸ Is there a parking space?

ihe demo niwa ga arimasu
❹ Is it furnished?

mochiron desu
❺ How much is the rent per month?

3 House

❶ なんてきれいな
タイルなん
でしょう！
*nante kireh na
tairu nandeshoh*

❷ 洗濯機は
ありますか？
*sentaku ki wa
arimasuka*

❸ 車庫は
ありますか？
shako wa arimasuka

❹ 家具付きですか？
kagu tsuki desuka

❺ 家賃は一月いくら
ですか？
*yachin wa hitotsuki
ikura desuka*

4 At home (3 minutes)

Say the Japanese for the following items.

❶ washing machine
❷ sofa
❸ attic
❹ dining room
❺ tree
❻ garden

❽ table

4 At home

❶ 洗濯機
sentaku ki

❷ ソファ
sofa

❸ 屋根裏
yane ura

❹ ダイニング
ルーム
dainingu ru-mu

❺ 木
ki

❻ 庭
niwa

YU-BIN KYOKU TO GINKOH
Post office and bank

1 Warm up (1 minute)

Ask "How do I get to the station?", and "Where's the post office?" (pp.50-1 and pp.68-9)

What's the Japanese for passport? (pp.54-5)

Ask "What time is it?" (pp.30-1)

Postcards are a popular form of letter in Japan, especially when sending a New Year greeting. Some postcards are prepaid (the bird and flower pictures work as stamps), so you can post them as soon as you write them.

2 Words to remember: post (3 minutes)

手紙 *tegami*	letter	
封筒 *fu-toh*	envelope	
小包 *kozutsumi*	parcel	
エアメール *ea mehru*	air mail	
書留郵便 *kakidome yu-bin*	registered post	
切手 *kitte*	stamps	
郵便配達人 *yu-bin haitatsu nin*	postman	
ポスト *posuto*	post box	

Familiarize yourself with these words and test yourself using the cover flap to conceal the Japanese on the left.

はがき
hagaki
postcard

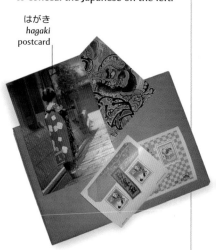

3 In conversation (3 minutes)

トラベラーズチェックを両替したいです。
toraberahzu chekku o ryohgae shitai desu

I'd like to change some traveller's cheques.

身分証明書をお持ちですか？
mibun shohmehsho o omochi desuka

Do you have any identification?

はい、これがパスポートです。
hai, kore ga pasupohto desu

Yes, here's my passport.

クレジットカード
kurejitto kahdo
credit card

クレジットカードで
払えますか？
kurejitto kahdo de harae masuka
Can I pay with a credit card?

4 Words to remember: bank (2 minutes)

Familiarize yourself with these words and test yourself using the cover flap to conceal the Japanese on the right.

money	お金 *okane*
traveller's cheques	トラベラーズチェック *toraberahzu chekku*
cashier	窓口 *madoguchi*
notes	紙幣 *shiheh*
coins	硬貨 *kohka*
cashpoint	ATM *"ATM"*
exchange rate	レート *rehto*

5 Useful phrases (4 minutes)

Learn these phrases and then test yourself using the cover flap.

I'd like to change some money.	お金を両替したいです。 *okane o ryohgae shitai desu*
What is the exchange rate?	レートはいくらですか？ *rehto wa ikura desuka*
Where's the cashpoint?	ATMはどこですか？ *"ATM" wa doko desuka*

6 Say it (2 minutes)

I'd like to change some dollars.

Here's my credit card.

Where's the post box?

ここにご署名をお願いします。
koko ni goshomeh o onegai shimasu

Please sign here.

どんな紙幣をご希望ですか？
donna shihei o gokiboh desuka

How would you like the notes?

五千円札をお願い
します。
go-sen-yen satsu o onegai shimasu

5000-yen notes, please.

What is the Japanese for "The fridge is broken"? (pp.100-1)

What's the Japanese for "today" and "tomorrow"? (pp.28-9)

Say "Thank you very much". (pp.40-1)

SHU-RI
Repairs

You can combine the Japanese words on these pages with the vocabulary you learned in week 10 to help you explain basic problems and cope with arranging most repairs. Rented accommodation is usually arranged via *agents*, known as **fudohsanya**. They can also help with problems.

2 Words to remember (4 minutes)

Familiarize yourself with these words and test yourself using the flap.

配管工 *haikankoh*	plumber
電気技師 *denki gishi*	electrician
機械技師 *kikai gishi*	mechanic
建築家 *kenchiku ka*	builder
大工 *daiku*	carpenter
コンピューター修理店 *konpyu-tah shu-ri ten*	computer repair shop
清掃業者 *seisoh gyohsha*	cleaner
コック *kokku*	cook

機械技師は必要ないです。
kikai gishi wa hitsuyoh nai desu
I don't need a mechanic.

3 In conversation (3 minutes)

おはようございます。
山田ですが。
ohayoh gozaimasu.
Yamada desuga

Good morning.
This is Mrs Yamada.

おはようございます。
どうかなさいましたか？
ohayoh gozaimasu.
dohka nasai mashitaka

Good morning. Is there anything wrong?

食器洗い機が壊れて
います。
shokki araiki ga
kowarete imasu

The dishwasher is broken.

4 Useful phrases (3 minutes)

Learn these phrases and then test yourself using the cover flap.

Please clean the bathroom.	バスルームを掃除 してください。 *basu ru-mu o sohji* *shite kudasai*
Can you repair the television?	テレビを修理して もらえますか？ *terebi o shu-ri shite* *mora-e masuka*
Can you recommend a good mechanic?	良い修理屋を紹介 してもらえますか？ *ih shu-ri ya o shohkai* *shite mora-e masuka*

これはどこで修理してもらえ
ますか？
kore wa doko de shu-ri shite
mora-e masuka
Where can I get this repaired?

5 Put into practice (4 minutes)

Cover up the text on the right and complete the dialogue in Japanese.

CDドライブが壊れています。
CD doraibu ga
kowarete imasu

Your CD drive is broken.

Ask: Can you recommend a good computer repair shop?

良いコンピューター修理店
を紹介してもらえますか？
ih konpyu-tah shu-ri
ten o shohkai shite
mora-e masuka

街に一店あります。
machi ni itten arimasu

There's one in the town.

どうもありがとう
ございます。
dohmo arigatoh gozaimasu

Say: Thank you very much.

今日中に修理できる
でしょう。
kyohjyu-ni shu-ri dekiru deshoh
It's possible to repair it today.

修理担当者を送ります。
shu-ri tantoh sha
o okuri masu

We'll send a repair man.

今日中に来てくれ
ますか？
kyohjyu ni kite kure masuka

Can you do it today?

すみません。明日の朝に
なります。
sumimasen. ashita no asa
ni narimasu

Sorry. But it will be tomorrow morning.

KURU
To come

Say the days of the week in Japanese. (pp.28-9)

How do you say "cleaner"? (pp.110-11)

Say "It's 9.30", "10.45", and "12.00". (pp.30-1)

Japanese verbs don't generally change with the subject, but do take different endings according to the tense or "mood" (see pp.40-1). Below you will see some of these changes for the verb *kuru* (*to come*) with examples, including the useful *ki-te* form used for invitations.

2 **Useful phrases** (6 minutes)

Say the different forms of *kuru* (*to come*) aloud. Use the cover flap to test yourself and, when you are confident, practice the sample sentences below.

来る *kuru*	to come (infinitive)
来ます *kimasu*	come/coming (present)
来ません *kimasen*	not come/coming (present negative)
来ました *kimashita*	came (past)
来ませんでした *kimasen deshita*	didn't come (past negative)
来て *ki-te*	come! (invitation)
バスが来ません。 *basu ga kimasen*	The bus isn't coming.
大工さんは九時に 来ました。 *daikusan wa kuji ni kimashita*	The carpenter came at nine o'clock.
清掃業者は今日は 来ませんでした。 *sehsoh gyohsha wa kyoh wa kimasen deshita*	The cleaner didn't come today.
明日来るつもりです。 *ashita kuru tsumori desu*	I intend to come tomorrow.

彼らは電車で来ます。
karera wa densha de kimasu
They're coming by train.

Conversational tip Beware of English phrases using *come* that translate differently in Japanese. For example, the Japanese equivalent of *I come from Australia* would be *ohsutoraria jin desu*, which translates literally as *Australia person I am*.

3 Invitations (4 minutes)

You can use *ki-te* (*come!*) with *kudasai* (*please*) for basic invitations, but there are also different expressions depending on the level of formality.

Please come to my birthday party.	私の誕生パーティーに来てください。 *watashi no tanjyoh pahtih ni ki-te kudasai*
Can you come to our reception on Monday? (formal)	月曜日のレセプションにいらしていただけますか？ *getsuyoh-bi no resepushon ni irashite itadake masuka*
Would you be able to come to our seminar on Friday? (very formal)	金曜日のセミナーにお越し願えますでしょうか？ *kinyoh-bi no seminah ni okoshi negaemasu deshohka*
Come to my dinner party! (informal)	ディナーパーティーに来てね！ *dinah pahtih ni kitene*

4 Put into practice (4 minutes)

Join in this conversation. Read the Japanese on the left and follow the instructions to make your reply. Then test yourself by concealing the answers with the cover flap.

もしもし。
moshi moshi

Hello.

Say: Hello. Please come to my birthday party.

もしもし。私の誕生パーティーに来てください。
moshi moshi. watashi no tanjyoh pahtih ni ki-te kudasai

パーティーはいつですか？
pahtih wa itsu desuka

When is the party?

Say: It's tomorrow at eight o'clock.

明日の8時です。
ashitano hachi ji desu

はい、ぜひ。
hai, zehi

Yes, I'd love to.

Say: So see you tomorrow.

ではまたあした。
dewa mata ashita

KEHSATSU TO HANZAI
Police and crime

1 **Warm up** (1 minute)

What's the Japanese for "tall" and "short"? (pp.64–5)

Say "The room is big" and "The bed is small". (pp.64–5)

Japanese police cars are black and white with a red strip light on the roof. The uniforms are blue and grey with a peaked cap. Note that the terms *otoko* (man) and *onna* (woman) in section 4 are not very polite as they refer to criminal suspects. More polite equivalents would be *danseh* and *jyoseh*.

2 **Words to remember: crime** (4 minutes)

Familiarize yourself with these words.

どろぼう *doroboh*	thief/burglar
通報 *tsuh-hoh*	police report
報告書 *hohkoku sho*	statement
証人 *shoh nin*	witness
目撃者 *mokugeki sha*	eyewitness
弁護士 *bengo shi*	lawyer
警察官 *kehsatsu kan*	police officer

弁護士が必要です。
bengo shi ga hitsuyoh desu
I need a lawyer.

3 **Useful phrases** (3 minutes)

Learn these phrases and then test yourself using the cover flap.

すられました。 *surare mashita*	I've been pick-pocketed.
何が盗まれましたか？ *nani ga nusumare mashitaka*	What was stolen?
犯人を見ましたか？ *hannin o mimashitaka*	Did you see who did it?
いつおこり ましたか？ *itsu okori mashitaka*	When did it happen?

カメラ
kamera
camera

お金
okane
money

財布
saifu
wallet

4 Words to remember: appearance (5 minutes)

Learn these words and then test yourself using the cover flap.

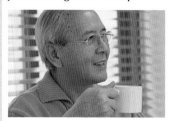

男は白髪混じりで眼鏡をかけていました。
otoko wa shiraga majiri de megane
o kakete imashita
The man had grey hair and glasses.

女は背が高く髪が長かったです。
onna wa se ga takaku kami ga
nagakatta desu
The woman was tall and had long hair.

man/men	男	*otoko*
woman/women	女	*onna*
tall	背の高い	*se no takai*
short	背の低い	*se no hikui*
young	若い	*wakai*
old	年を取った	*toshi o totta*
fat	太った	*futotta*
thin	痩せた	*yaseta*
beard	あごひげ	*ago hige*
moustache	口ひげ	*kuchi hige*
glasses	眼鏡	*megane*

Read it The Japanese script for *police* is written with two *kanji* characters: 警察 (*kehsatsu*). Adding the character 官 (*kan*) will produce *policeman*: 警察官 (*kehsatsu kan*); and adding 署 (*sho*) will produce *police station*: 警察署 (*kehsatsu sho*).

5 Put into practice (2 minutes)

Practice these phrases. Then use the cover flap to hide the text on the right and follow the instructions to make your reply in Japanese.

男はどんな格好でしたか？
otoko wa donna kakkoh
deshita ka

Can you describe him?

Say: He was short and fat.

背が低く太っていました。
se ga hikuku futotte
imashita

髪は？
kami wa

And the hair?

Say: He had grey hair and a beard.

白髪であごひげを生やして
いました。
shiraga de ago hige
o hayashite imashita

Kotae
Answers (Cover with flap)

FUKUSHU TO KURIKAESHI
Review and repeat

1 To come

❶ 私はバスで来ます。
watashi wa basu de kimasu

❷ 電気技師は昨日来ました。
denki gishi wa kinoh kimashita

❸ 私の誕生パーティーに来てください。
watashi no tanjyoh pahtih ni ki-te kudasai

❹ 清掃業者は木曜日には来ませんでした。
sehsoh gyohsha wa mokuyoh bi niwa kimasen deshita

1 To come (3 minutes)

Put the following sentences into Japanese using the correct form of *kuru* (to come).

❶ I'm coming by bus.

❷ The electrician came yesterday.

❸ Please come to my birthday party.

❹ The cleaner didn't come on Thursday.

2 Bank and post

❶ クレジットカード
kurejitto kahdo

❷ 紙幣
shiheh

❸ はがき
hagaki

❹ 小包
kozutsumi

❺ 切手
kitte

2 Bank and post (4 minutes)

Name the numbered items in Japanese.

credit card ❶

❷ banknotes

❸ postcard

❹ parcel

❺ stamps

3 Appearance (4 minutes)

What do these descriptions mean?

❶ *se ga hikuku yasete imashita*

❷ *otoko wa shohto katto deshita*

❸ *onna wa megane o kakete imashita*

❹ *otoko wa kichi hige o hayashite imashita*

❺ *otoko wa shiraga de ago hige o hayashite imashita*

3 Appearance

❶ *He was short and thin.*

❷ *The man had short hair.*

❸ *The woman had glasses.*

❹ *The man had a moustache.*

❺ *He had grey hair and a beard.*

4 The pharmacy (4 minutes)

You are asking a pharmacist for advice. Join in the conversation, replying in Japanese where you see the numbered English prompts.

konnichiwa. doh shimashitaka
❶ I have a stomachache.

kaze gimi desuka
❷ No, but I have a headache.

kore o onomi kudasai
❸ Do you have that as a syrup?

hai, arimasu
❹ How much is that?

happyaku yen ni narimasu
❺ Thank you.

4 The pharmacy

❶ 腹痛がします。
fukutsu ga shimasu

❷ いいえ、でも頭痛がします。
ihe, demo zutsu ga shimasu

❸ それのシロップはありますか？
sore no shiroppu wa arimasuka

❹ いくらですか？
ikura desuka

❺ ありがとう。
arigatoh

REJYAH
Leisure time

What is the Japanese for "museum" and "cinema"? (pp.48-9)

Say "I like the pond". (p.103)

Ask "What's your profession?" (pp.78-9)

Popular leisure activities outside the house include shopping, playing in the ubiquitous and often very large arcades, or going to karaoke "boxes". New theme parks open regularly and are popular with adults and children alike. Sumo is popular with older people, but theatre and opera are minority pursuits.

2 **Words to remember** (4 minutes)

Familiarize yourself with these words and test yourself using the cover flap to conceal the Japanese on the left.

劇場 *gekijyoh*	theatre
映画 *eiga*	cinema/film
テーマパーク *tehma pahku*	theme park
音楽 *ongaku*	music
アート *ahto*	art
スポーツ *supohtsu*	sport
旅行 *ryokoh*	travelling
読書 *dokusho*	reading

歌舞伎が大好きです。
kabuki ga daisuki desu
I love Kabuki theatre.

セット
setto
set

3 **In conversation** (4 minutes)

カラオケに行きませんか？
karaoke ni ikimasenka

Do you want to go to a karaoke bar?

カラオケはきらいです。
karaoke wa kirai desu

I don't really like karaoke.

暇なときは何をしていますか？
hima na toki wa nani o shite imasuka

What do you do in your free time?

ビデオゲームが好きです。
bideo gehmu ga suki desu
I like video games.

俳優
haiyu
actor

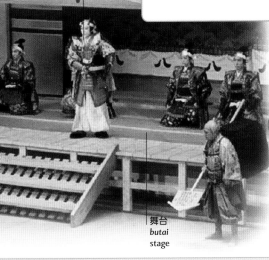

舞台
butai
stage

4 Useful phrases (4 minutes)

Learn these phrases and then test yourself using the cover flap.

What do you do in your free time? (formal)	暇なときは何をしていますか？ *hima na toki wa nani o shite imasuka*
What do you do in your free time? (informal)	暇なとき何してる？ *hima na toki nani shiteru*
My hobby is reading.	趣味は読書です。 *shumi wa dokusho desu*
I prefer the cinema.	私は映画の方が好きです。 *watashi wa eiga no hohga sukidesu*
I hate opera.	私はオペラは大嫌いです。 *watashi wa opera wa daikirai desu*

5 Say it (2 minutes)

I like music.

I prefer art.

My hobby is opera.

I hate theme parks.

ショッピングが好きです。
shoppingu ga suki desu

I like shopping.

私はショッピングは大嫌いです。
watashi wa shoppingu wa daikirai desu

I hate shopping.

良いですよ。一人で行きます。
ihdesuyo. hitori de ikimasu

No problem, I'll go on my own.

SUPOHTSU TO SHUMI
Sport and hobbies

What's the Japanese for "fish"? (pp.104-5)

Say "I like the theatre" and "I prefer travelling". (pp.118-19)

Say "I don't really like...". (pp.118-19)

Traditional Japanese sports include wrestling, martial arts, and fishing. These are still popular, but football, baseball, and golf have also established themselves. Arts and crafts include flower arranging, silk-screen painting, and calligraphy. Participating in tea ceremonies is also a popular hobby.

2 **Words to remember** (5 minutes)

Memorize these words and then test yourself.

サッカー *sakkah*	football
野球 *yakyu*	baseball
テニス *tenisu*	tennis
水泳 *suiei*	swimming
登山 *tozan*	mountain climbing
魚釣り *sakana tsuri*	fishing
絵を描くこと *e o kaku koto*	painting
習字 *syu-ji*	calligraphy

バンカー
bankah
bunker

ゴルファー
gorufah
golfer

毎日ゴルフをします。
mainichi gorufu o shimasu
I play golf every day.

3 **Useful phrases** (2 minutes)

Familiarize yourself with these phrases.

野球をします。 *yakyu o shimasu*	I play baseball.
彼はテニスをします。 *kare wa tenisu o shimasu*	He plays tennis.
彼女は絵を描くことが好きです。 *kanojyo wa e o kaku koto ga suki desu*	She likes painting.

4 Phrases to remember (4 minutes)

Learn the phrases below and then test yourself.
Notice that *I play* is *shimasu* for sports, but
hikimasu for musical instruments.

What do you like doing? (formal)	何をするのがお好きですか？ *nani o surunoga* *osuki desuka*
What do you like doing? (informal)	何をするのが好き？ *nani o surunoga suki*
I like playing golf.	ゴルフをするのが好きです。 *gorufu o surunoga suki desu*
I like playing baseball.	野球をするのが好きです。 *yakyu o surunoga suki desu*
I play tennis.	テニスをします。 *tenisu o shimasu*
I like going fishing.	私は魚釣りが好きです。 *watashi wa sakana tsuri ga* *suki desu*
I go mountain climbing.	登山に行きます。 *tozan ni ikimasu*

バイオリンを弾きます。
baiorin o hikimasu
I play the violin.

―――― フラッグ
furaggu
flag

―――― ゴルフコース
gorufu kohsu
golf course

5 Put into practice (3 minutes)

Learn these phrases. Then cover up the text on the right and complete
the dialogue in Japanese. Check your answers.

何をするのがお好き
ですか？
nani o surunoga osuki desuka

What do you like doing?

Say: Playing football.

サッカーするのが
好きです。
sakkah surunoga
suki desu

野球もなさいますか？
yakyu mo nasai masuka

Do you play baseball
as well?

Say: No, I play golf.

いいえ、ゴルフをします。
ihe, gorufu o shimasu

よくプレーなさいますか？
yoku pureh nasai masuka

Do you play often?

Say: Every week.

毎週です。
maishu desu

SHAKOHTEKI NA BAMEN DE
Socializing

As a business guest, it's more common to be invited to a restaurant than to someone's home. This is partly practical - people often have long commutes. But if you're staying for longer, you may be invited for a meal or a party.

1 Warm up (1 minute)

Say "(your) husband" and "(your) wife". (pp.12-13)

How do you say "lunch" and "dinner" in Japanese? (pp.20-1)

Say "Sorry, I'm busy that day". (pp.32-3)

2 Useful phrases (3 minutes)

Learn these phrases and then test yourself.

ディナーにいらっしゃいませんか？ *dinah ni irasshai masenka*	Would you like to come for dinner?
水曜日はいかがですか？ *suiyoh bi wa ikaga desuka*	What about Wednesday?
また今度誘ってください。 *mata kondo sasotte kudasai*	Perhaps another time.

Cultural tip When visiting a Japanese home, remember that it's usual to remove your outdoor shoes at the door. Take a gift for the host or hostess. Flowers, a bottle of drink, or a present from your home country will be very appreciated.

3 In conversation (6 minutes)

火曜日のディナーにいらっしゃいませんか？
kayoh bi no dinah ni irasshai masenka?

Would you like to come for dinner on Tuesday?

すみません。火曜日は忙しいです。
sumimasen. kayoh bi wa isogashih desu

Sorry. I'm busy on Tuesday.

木曜日はいかがですか？
mokuyoh bi wa ikaga desuka

What about Thursday?

4 Words to remember (3 minutes)

Familiarize yourself with these words and test yourself using the flap.

party	パーティー *pahtih*
invitation	招待 *shohtai*
gift	お土産 *omiyage*

招待者
shohtai sha
hostess

お客
okyaku
guest

ご招待ありがとう
ございます。
goshohtai arigatoh gozaimasu
Thank you for inviting us.

Read it You can now distinguish the three Japanese character sets and recognize some basic recurring words. Use the tables on pp.158-9 to look back over the lessons and see how much more you can read.

5 Put into practice (2 minutes)

Join in this conversation.

土曜日にパーティーを開く
のですが、お暇ですか？
*doyoh bi ni pahtih o hiraku
no desuga, ohima desuka*

We are having a party on Saturday. Are you free?

Say: Yes, how nice!

はい、素敵ですね！
hai, suteki desune

ああよかった！
ah yokatta

That's great!

Say: At what time should we arrive?

何時に伺い
ましょうか？
nanji ni ukagai mashohka

はい、素敵ですね！
hai, suteki desune

Yes, how nice!

ご主人もご一緒に。
goshujin mo goissho ni

Please bring your husband.

何時に伺いましょうか？
nanji ni ukagai mashohka

At what time should we arrive?

FUKUSHU TO KURIKAESHI
Review and repeat

1 Animals

❶ 猫
neko

❷ 鳥
tori

❸ 馬
uma

❹ 魚
sakana

❺ 犬
inu

1 Animals (3 minutes)

Name the numbered animals in Japanese.

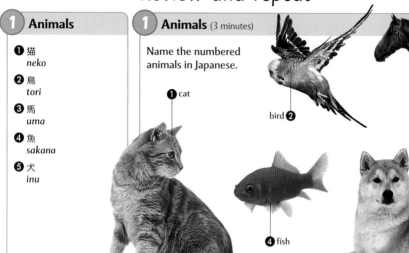

❶ cat

bird ❷

❹ fish

2 I like...

❶ 野球をするのが好き
です。
*yakyu o surunoga
suki desu*

❷ ゴルフをするのが好き
です。
*gorufu o surunoga
suki desu*

❸ 私は絵を描くことが
好きです。
*watashi wa e o kaku
koto ga suki desu*

2 I like... (4 minutes)

Say the following in Japanese:

❶ I like playing baseball.
❷ I like playing golf.
❸ I like painting.

Kotae
Answers (Cover with flap)

❸ horse

❺ dog

3 Leisure (4 minutes)

What do these Japanese sentences mean?

❶ *karaoke wa daikirai desu*

❷ *bideo gehmu ga suki desu*

❸ *shumi wa dokusho desu*

❹ *watashi wa gekijyoh no hohga sukidesu*

❺ *baiorin o hikimasu*

3 Leisure

❶ *I hate karaoke.*

❷ *I like video games.*

❸ *My hobby is reading.*

❹ *I prefer the theatre.*

❺ *I play the violin.*

4 An invitation (4 minutes)

You are invited for dinner. Join in the conversation, replying in Japanese following the English prompts.

doyoh bi no dinah ni irasshai masenka

❶ Sorry, I'm busy on Saturday.

mokuyoh bi wa ikaga desuka

❷ Yes, how nice!

goshujin mo goissho ni

❸ At what time should we arrive?

ichi ji han dewa

❹ Thank you very much.

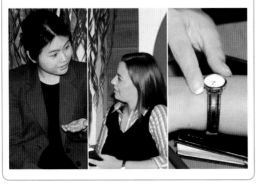

4 An invitation

❶ すみません。
土曜日は忙しいです。
sumimasen. doyoh bi wa isogashih desu

❷ はい、素敵
ですね！
hai, suteki desune

❸ 何時に伺いましょう
か？
nanji ni ukagai mashohka

❹ ありがとうございます。
arigatoh gozaimasu

Reinforce and progress

Regular practice is the key to maintaining and advancing your language skills. In this section you will find a variety of suggestions for reinforcing and extending your knowledge of Japanese. Many involve returning to exercises in the book and using the dictionary to extend their scope. Go back through the lessons in a different order, mix and match activities to make up your own 15-minute daily programme, or focus on topics that are of particular relevance to your current needs.

1 Warm up (1 minute)

Ask "How much is that?" (pp.18-19)

What are "breakfast", "lunch", and "dinner"? (pp.20-1)

What are "three", "four", "five", and "six"? (pp.10-11)

Keep warmed up
Re-visit the Warm Up boxes to remind yourself of key words and phrases. Make sure you work your way through all of them on a regular basis.

2 I'd like... (3 minutes)

Say "I'd like" the following:

❹ tea
cake ❶
sugar ❷
coffee ❸

Review and repeat again
Work through a Review and Repeat lesson as a way of reinforcing words and phrases presented in the course. Return to the main lesson for any topic on which you are no longer confident.

3 In conversation: taxi (2 minutes)

Carry on conversing
Re-read the In Conversation panels. Say both parts of the conversation, paying attention to the pronunciation. Where possible, try incorporating new words from the dictionary.

秋葉原までお願いします。
Akihabara ma-de onegai shimasu

To Akihabara, please.

わかりました。
wakarimashita

Very well.

ここで降ろしてください。
kokode oroshite kudasai

Can you drop me here, please?

4 Useful phrases (3 minutes)

Learn these phrases and then test yourself using the cover flap.

What time do you open?	何時に開きますか？ *nanji ni akimasuka*
What time does the shop close?	店は何時に閉まりますか？ *mise wa nanji ni shimari masuka*
Is wheelchair access possible?	車いすは使えますか？ *kurumaisu wa tsukae masuka*

Practice phrases
Return to the Useful Phrases and Put into Practice exercises. Test yourself using the cover flap. When you are confident, devise your own versions of the phrases, using new words from the dictionary.

Match, repeat, and extend

Remind yourself of words related to specific topics by returning to the Match and Repeat and Words to Remember exercises. Test yourself using the cover flap. Discover new words in that subject area by referring to the dictionary and menu guide.

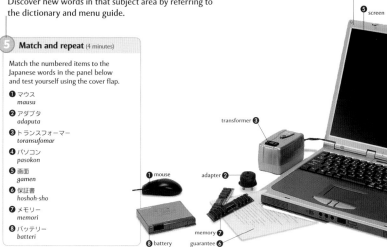

5 Match and repeat (4 minutes)

Match the numbered items to the Japanese words in the panel below and test yourself using the cover flap.

1 マウス
mausu

2 アダプタ
adaputa

3 トランスフォーマー
toransufomar

4 パソコン
pasokon

5 画面
gamen

6 保証書
hoshoh-sho

7 メモリー
memori

8 バッテリー
batteri

4 laptop
5 screen
transformer **3**
1 mouse
adapter **2**
memory **7**
8 battery
guarantee **6**

Say it again

The Say it exercises are a useful instant reminder for each lesson. Practise these, using your own vocabulary variations from the dictionary or elsewhere in the lesson.

6 Say it (2 minutes)

What kind of flower is this?

I like the waterfall.

Is there a pond?

Using other resources

In addition to working with this book, try the following language extension ideas:

Visit Japan, if you can, and try out your new skills with native speakers. Otherwise, find out if there is a Japanese community near you. There may be shops, cafés, restaurants, and clubs. Try to visit some of these and use your Japanese to order food and drink and strike up conversations. Most native speakers will be happy to speak Japanese to you.

Join a language class or club. There are usually evening and day classes available at a variety of different levels. Or you could start a club yourself if you have friends who are also interested in keeping up their Japanese.

Practise your new knowledge of the Japanese scripts and characters (see pp.158-9). Look at the back of food packages and other products. You will often find a Japanese list of ingredients or components. See if you can spot some familiar words in the Japanese list and then compare to the English equivalent.

Look at the titles and advertisements of Japanese magazines and manga comics. The pictures will help you to decipher the script. Look for familiar words and characters, even if you can't make out the whole text.

Use the internet to find websites for learning languages, some of which offer free online help.

MENU GUIDE

This guide lists the most common terms you may encounter on Japanese menus. Dishes are divided into categories and the Japanese script is displayed clearly to help you identify items on a menu.

Starters and soups

hamu	ハム	ham
ohdoburu	オードブル	hors d'oeuvres
otsumami	おつまみ	Japanese appetizer
tsukidashi	つきだし	Japanese appetizer
ise-ebi	伊勢えび	lobster
meron	メロン	melon
minestorohne	ミネストローネ	minestrone
kuruma-ebi	車えび	prawns
smohku sahmon	スモークサーモン	smoked salmon
misoshiru	みそ汁	soup made with fermented bean paste
tomato supu	トマトスープ	tomato soup

Egg dishes

behkon-eggu	ベーコンエッグ	bacon and eggs
tamago	卵	egg
medama-yaki	目玉焼き	fried eggs
hamu-eggu	ハムエッグ	ham and eggs
tamago-yaki	玉子焼き	Japanese omelette
omuretsu	オムレツ	omelette
omuraisu	オムライス	rolled omelette filled with rice

chawan-mushi	茶碗蒸し	savoury "custard" with egg and fish
tamago-dohfu	卵豆腐	steamed egg and tofu

Fish and sushi

awabi	あわび	abalone
suzuki	すずき／鱸	sea bass
fugu	フグ/河豚	blowfish
katsuo	かつお／鰹	bonito, tunny
unajyu	うな重	broiled eel on rice
koi	コイ／鯉	carp
nami	並	cheaper selection of fish
hamaguri	はまぐり／蛤	clam
tara	タラ／鱈	cod
tarako	タラコ	cod roe
anago	あなご	conger eel
kani	かに／蟹	crab
unagi	うなぎ／鰻	eel
joh	上	expensive selection
unadon	うな丼	grilled eel on rice
nishin	にしん／鰊	herring
kazunoko	かずのこ	herring roe
aji	あじ／鯵	horse mackerel
saba	さば／鯖	mackerel
gomoku-zushi	五目寿司	mixed sushi
chirashi-zushi	ちらし寿司	mixed sushi on rice

tako	たこ／蛸	octopus
oshi-zushi	押し寿司	Osaka-style sushi cut in squares
kaki	カキ／牡蠣	oyster
sashimi	刺身	raw fish
sushi	寿司／すし	raw fish on riceballs
nigiri-zushi	にぎり寿司	raw fish on riceballs
sake	さけ／鮭	salmon
ikura	イクラ	salmon roe
iwashi	いわし／鰯	sardines
hotategai	ホタテ貝	scallop
tai	タイ／鯛	sea bream
kappa-maki	カッパ巻き	seasoned rice and cucumber wrapped in seaweed
inari-zushi	いなり寿司	seasoned rice wrapped in fried tofu
uni	うに	sea urchin
ebi	えび／海老	shrimp
nori-maki	のり巻き	sliced roll of rice, vegetables, and fish powder, wrapped in seaweed
ika	イカ	squid
ayu	あゆ／鮎	sweet smelt
masu	マス／鱒	trout
maguro	まぐろ／鮪	tuna
kujira	くじら／鯨	whale
buri	ブリ／鰤	yellowtail

Meat and poultry

bahbekyu	バーベキュー	barbecue
gyu-niku	牛肉	beef
bihfu	ビーフ	beef
teppan-yaki	鉄板焼き	beef and vegetables grilled at the table
gyu-shohgayaki	牛しょうが焼き	beef cooked in soy sauce with ginger
bihfu-sutehki	ビーフステーキ	beef steak
niwatori	鶏	chicken
abaraniku	あばら肉	chops/ribs
korokke	コロッケ	croquettes
tonkatsu	とんかつ	deep-fried pork cutlets
katsudon	カツ丼	deep-fried pork cutlet on rice
kamo	鴨	duck
hireniku	ひれ肉	fillet
yakiniku	焼肉	fried pork marinated in soy sauce
kushiyaki	串焼き	grilled meat or vegetables on skewers
hanbahgah	ハンバーガー	hamburger
rebah	レバー	liver
niku	肉	meat
nikudango	肉団子	meat-filled dumplings
honetsuki	骨付き	on the bone
butaniku	豚肉	pork

buta-shohgayaki	豚しょうが焼き	pork cooked in soy sauce with ginger
uzura	うずら	quail
kareh-raisu	カレーライス	rice with curry-flavoured stew
rohsuto-bihfu	ローストビーフ	roast beef
rohsuto-chikin	ローストチキン	roast chicken
rohsuto-pohku	ローストポーク	roast pork
sohsehji	ソーセージ	sausage
sahroin	サーロイン	sirloin
yakitori	焼き鳥	skewered chicken cooked over a grill
shabu-shabu	しゃぶしゃぶ	sliced beef with vegetables boiled in a pot at the table
sukiyaki	すき焼き	sliced beef with vegetables cooked at the table
spearibu	スペアリブ	spare ribs
suzume	すずめ	sparrow
stehki	ステーキ	steak

Rice dishes

...domburi	… 丼	bowl of rice with something on top
unagidon	うなぎ丼	*domburi* with grilled eel
oyakodon	親子丼	*domburi* with chicken and egg
tendon	天丼	*domburi* with deep-fried seafood

tamagodon	卵丼	*domburi* cooked in egg with onions
chyukadon	中華丼	*domburi* with pork and vegetables
nikudon	肉丼	*domburi* with sliced beef
katsudon	カツ丼	*domburi* with deep-fried breaded pork cutlet
chah-han	チャーハン	fried rice
gohan/raisu	ご飯／ライス	rice
kamameshi	釜飯	rice steamed in fish stock with pieces of meat, fish, and vegetable
chikin raisu	チキンライス	rice with chicken
onigiri	おにぎり	rice balls wrapped in seaweed

Noodle dishes

rahmen	ラーメン	Chinese noodles
chahshumen	チャーシューメン	Chinese noodles in pork stock
chanpon	ちゃんぽん	Chinese noodles in salted stock with meat and vegetables
kanton-men	広東麺	Chinese noodles in salted pork-flavoured soup with vegetables
soba	そば	long, brownish buckwheat noodles
udon	うどん	long, thick, white wheatflour noodles

sohmen	そうめん	long, thin, white wheatflour noodles (usually served cold in the summer)
wantan-men	ワンタンメン	noodle squares (wanton) containing ground pork and leeks, served in soup
tempura soba	天ぷらそば	noodles in fish stock with deep-fried shrimps
tsukimi soba	月見そば	noodles in fish stock with raw egg on top
niku udon	肉うどん	noodles in fish stock with pork or beef
kake soba	かけそば	simple dish of noodles in fish broth
kitsune udon	きつねうどん	noodles in fish broth with fried bean curd
chikara udon	力うどん	noodles in fish broth with rice cake (mochi)
moyashi soba	もやしそば	noodles in pork broth with bean sprouts
mori soba	盛りそば	noodles served cold, with sweetened soy sauce dip
miso rahmen	味噌ラーメン	noodles and pork in bean paste broth
gomoku soba	五目そば	soba noodles in broth with pieces of vegetable and meat

Vegetables, seasonings, and salads

aspara	アスパラ	asparagus
nasu	なす	aubergine
takenoko	竹の子	bamboo shoots
tohfu	豆腐	bean curd, tofu
mame	豆	beans
ohitashi	おひたし	boiled spinach with seasoning
kyabetsu	キャベツ	cabbage
ninjin	にんじん	carrot
kyu-ri	キュウリ	cucumber
miso	味噌	fermented soyabean paste
nattoh	納豆	fermented soyabeans
abura-age	油揚げ	fried bean curd
shohga	しょうが	ginger
pihman	ピーマン	green pepper
matsutake	松茸	Japanese mushrooms
nori	海苔	dried seaweed
retasu	レタス	lettuce
mayonehzu	マヨネーズ	mayonnaise
masshurumu	マッシュルーム	mushrooms
kinoko	きのこ	mushrooms (general term)
karashi	からし	mustard
abura	油	oil
tamanegi	玉ねぎ	onion
poteto/jyagaimo	ポテト／ジャガイモ	potatoes
poteto sarada	ポテトサラダ	potato salad

sarada	サラダ	salad
shio	塩	salt
shiokarai	塩辛い	salty
shohyu	醤油	soy sauce
daizu	大豆	soyabeans
hohrensoh	ほうれん草	spinach
satoh	砂糖	sugar
amai	甘い	sweet
kohn	コーン	sweetcorn
tomato	トマト	tomato
yasai	野菜	vegetables
su	酢	vinegar
takuan	タクアン	yellow radish pickles

Japanese set meals

tehshoku	定食	set meal with rice, soup, pickle, and main dish
higawari	日替わり	*tehshoku* of the day
tempura	天ぷら	*tehshoku* with deep-fried prawns, seafood, or vegetables as the main dish
yakiniku	焼肉	*tehshoku* with grilled meat as the main dish
tonkatsu	とんかつ	*tehshoku* with battered and deep-fried pork cutlet as the main dish

sashimi	刺身	*tehshoku* with raw fish as the main dish
ohiru no	お昼の	lunchtime *tehshoku*
bentoh	弁当	boxed lunch (sold at railway stations, convenience stores, etc.)

Fruit and nuts

banana	バナナ	banana
cherih/sakurambo	チェリー／さくらんぼ	cherries
kuri	栗	chestnut
kokonattsu	ココナッツ	coconut
furu-tsu/kudamono	フルーツ／果物	fruit
gurehpu-furu-tsu	グレープフルーツ	grapefruit
remon	レモン	lemon
meron	メロン	melon
orenji	オレンジ	orange
pihchi/momo	ピーチ／桃	peach
kaki	柿	persimmon
painappuru	パイナップル	pineapple
kiichigo	ラズベリー／木苺	raspberry
sutoroberih/ichigo	ストロベリー／イチゴ	strawberries
mikan	みかん	tangerine
kurumi	クルミ	walnuts
suika	スイカ	watermelon

Desserts

appuru pai	アップルパイ	apple pie
kehki	ケーキ	cake
chihzu-kehki	チーズケーキ	cheesecake
chokorehto	チョコレート	chocolate
shu-kurihmu	シュークリーム	cream puff
kurehpu	クレープ	crêpe
uji-gohri	宇治氷	crushed ice with green tea syrup
kohri meron	氷メロン	crushed ice with melon syrup
dezahto	デザート	dessert
dohnatsu	ドーナツ	doughnut
mitsumame	みつ豆	gelatine cubes and sweet beans with pieces of fruit
aisukurihmu	アイスクリーム	ice cream
zerih	ゼリー	jelly
mochi	もち	rice cakes (soft and glutinous when ready to eat)
senbeh	せんべい	rice crackers
manjyu	まんじゅう	rice-flour buns with bean paste
shahbetto	シャーベット	sorbet
shohto kehki	ショートケーキ	"shortcake" (similar to sponge cake)
yohkan	ようかん	jelly with soft, sweet bean paste filling
sufure	スフレ	soufflé
kasutera	カステラ	sponge cake

sutoroberih aisukurihmu	ストロベリー アイスクリーム	strawberry ice cream
oshiruko	おしるこ	sweet bean soup with rice cake
purin	プリン	vanilla egg custard with brown sugar
banira aisukurihmu	バニラ アイスクリーム	vanilla ice cream
kurihmu anmitsu	クリームあんみつ	vanilla ice cream with seaweed jelly, sweet beans, and fruit
yohguruto	ヨーグルト	yoghurt

Western snacks

pan	パン	bread
batah	バター	butter
chihzu-rohru	チーズロール	cheese roll
furaido chikin	フライドチキン	fried chicken
hamusando	ハムサンド	ham sandwich
jamu	ジャム	jam
ranchi	ランチ	lunch
mahmarehdo	マーマレード	marmalade
piza	ピザ	pizza
sando icchi	サンドイッチ	sandwich
spagetti	スパゲッティ	spaghetti
tohsto	トースト	toast

Drinks

nomimono	飲み物	beverages
bihru	ビール	beer
kohcha	紅茶	black tea ("red tea")
kokoah	ココア	cocoa, hot chocolate
koh-hi	コーヒー	coffee
kohra	コーラ	cola
shohchyu	焼酎	Japanese vodka
nama bihru	生ビール	draught beer
sohda sui	ソーダ水	green, sweet, fizzy drink
ocha/ryokucha	お茶／緑茶	Japanese tea
remon tih	レモンティー	lemon tea
miruk/gyunyu	ミルク／牛乳	milk
miruku shehku	ミルクシェイク	milkshake
mineraru wohtah	ミネラルウォーター	mineral water
orenji jyu-su	オレンジジュース	orange juice
orenji sukasshu	オレンジスカッシュ	orange squash
pain jyu-su	パインジュース	pineapple juice
sake/nihon-shu	酒／日本酒	rice wine
saidah	サイダー	fizzy drink
miruku tih	ミルクティー	tea with milk
tomato jyu-su	トマトジュース	tomato juice
tonikku wohtah	トニック ウォーター	tonic water
uisukih	ウイスキー	whisky
onzarokku	オンザロック	(whisky) on the rocks
mizuwari	水割り	(whisky) with water

wain/budohshu	ワイン／ぶどう酒	wine
edamame	枝豆	green beans in the pod served as snacks with drinks

Chinese meals

subuta	酢豚	a kind of sweet-and-sour pork
mahboh-dohfu	マーボー豆腐	bean curd in spicy meat sauce mixture
chu-ka ryohri	中華料理	Chinese food
harumaki	春巻き	deep-fried spring roll
gyohza	餃子	fried dumplings stuffed with minced pork
kurage no	くらげの	sliced parboiled jellyfish
shu-mai	シュウマイ	small steamed pork dumplings in thin Chinese filo pastry
niku-man	肉まん	steamed dumplings filled with seasoned minced pork

Festival food

yaki-imo	焼き芋	baked sweet potato
watagashi	綿菓子	candy floss
ikayaki	イカ焼き	charcoal-grilled squid
takoyaki	たこ焼き	griddle-fried octopus (in batter)
oden	おでん	hotchpotch of fish and vegetable boiled in fish broth
amaguri	甘栗	roasted chestnuts
tohmorokoshi	とうもろこし	roasted corn on the cob
okonomiyaki	お好み焼き	Japanese-style savoury pancakes
tako senbeh	たこせんべい	shrimp-flavoured pink crackers

Cooking methods and styles

robatayaki	炉端焼き	charcoal-grilled fish and vegetables
okashi	お菓子	confectionery
kappoh	割烹	special order Japanese-style dishes
agemono	揚げ物	deep-fried foods
tempura	天ぷら	deep-fried seafood and vegetables in batter
nabemono	鍋物	food cooked in a pot at the table
yakimono	焼き物	grilled foods
kaiseki ryohri	懐石料理	Japanese haute cuisine
nihon ryohri/washoku	日本料理／和食	Japanese-style cuisine
men rui	麺類	noodle dishes

tsukemono	漬物	pickled foods
tori-ryohri	鳥料理	poultry dishes
kyohdo ryohri	郷土料理	regional specialities
gohan-mono	ご飯もの	rice dishes
nimono	煮物	simmered foods
shirumono	汁物	soups
mushimono	蒸し物	steamed foods
shohjin ryohri	精進料理	ascetic, monastic style of vegetarian cooking
sunomono	酢の物	vinegared foods
sehyoh ryohri	西洋料理	Western-style cuisine

DICTIONARY
English to Japanese

The plural is normally the same as the singular in Japanese. In general, Japanese descriptive words, or adjectives, may change depending on how they are used. Some of these adjectives are followed by *(no)* or *(na)*. If a noun is used following such a word then the *no* or *na* must be put after the adjective: *kanojo wa kireh desu* (she is pretty); *kanojo wa kireh na jyoseh desu* (she is a pretty girl).

A

about: about 16
  jyu-roku kurai
accelerator *akuseru*
accident *jiko*
accommodation *heya*
accountant *kaikehshi*
ache *itami*
actor *haiyu*
adapter (electrical)
  adaputa
address *jyu-sho*
admission charge
  nyujoh ryoh
aeroplane *hikohki*
after *ato*
afternoon *gogo*
aftershave lotion
  afutah-shehbu-rohshon
again *mata*
against *hantai*
agenda *kaigi jikoh*
air conditioning *eakon*
air freshener *ea-furesshnah*
air hostess *ea-hosutesu*
airline *kohku-gaisha*
air mail *ea mehru*
airport *ku-koh*
alcohol *arukohru*
all *zembu* **that's all, thanks**
  arigatoh, sore de zenbu desu
almost *hotondo*
alone *hitori de*
already *sudeni*
always *itsmo*
am: I am British
  watashi wa igirisu jin desu
ambulance *kyu-kyu-sha*
America *Amerika*
American (person) *amerika jin* (adj) *amerika no*
and (with nouns) *to*
  (with verbs) *soshite*
ankle *ashikubi*
anniversary *kinenbi*
anorak *anorakku*
another (different) *betsu (no)*
  (further) *moh hitotsu (no)*

answering machine
  rusuban denwa
antifreeze *futohzai*
antique shop *kottoh hin ten*
antiseptic *bohfuzai/ shohdokuzai*
apartment *apahto*
appetite *shokuyoku*
apple *ringo*
application form
  mohshkomisho
appointment *(go)yoyaku; apo*
apricot *anzu*
April *shi gatsu*
architecture (field of study)
  kenchiku gaku
are: you are very kind
  anata wa totemo shinsetsu desu **we are English**
  watashi tachi wa igirisu jin desu **they are Japanese**
  karera wa nihonjin desu
arm *ude*
arrivals *tohchaku*
art *ahto; bijutsu*
art gallery *bijutsukan*
artist *geijutsuka*
as: as soon as possible
  dekiru dake hayaku
ashtray *haizara*
Asia *Ajia*
asleep: he's asleep
  kare wa nemutte imasu
asthmatic: I'm asthmatic
  zensoku mochi desu
aspirin *aspirin*
at: at the post office
  yu-bin kyoku de
  at night *yoru*
  at 3 o'clock *san ji ni*
attic *yane ura*
attractive *miryokuteki (na)*
August *hachi gatsu*
aunt *oba(san)*
Australia *Ohsutoraria*
Australian (person)
  ohsutoraria jin
  (adj) *ohsutoraria no*

automatic *jidoh*
autumn *aki*
away: is it far away?
  tohi desuka **go away!**
  atchi e itte
awful *hidoi*
axe *ono*
axle *shajiku*

B

baby *akachan*
baby wipes *bebih waipu*
back *ushiro*
  (upper back, body) *senaka*
  (lower back, body) *koshi*
bacon *behkon*
  bacon and eggs
  behkon-eggu
bad *warui*
baker *pan ya*
balcony *barukonih*
ball *bohru* (dance) *butohkai*
ball-point pen *bohru-pen*
banana *banana*
band (musicians) *bando*
bandage *hohtai*
bank *ginkoh*
banknotes *shiheh*
bar *bah*
  bar of chocolate
  itachoko
barber *riyoh in*
bargain *bahgen*
baseball *yakyu*
basement *chika*
basin (sink) *sen-mendai*
basket *kago*
bath *ofuro/basu* **to have a bath** *ofuro ni hairu*
bathing hat *sui-ei boh*
bathroom *basu (ru-mu); ofuroba*
battery *batteri; denchi*
beach *hamabe/kaigan*
beans *mame*
beard *hige*
beautiful *utsukushih*
beauty products *keshoh hin*

because (da)kara
   because it is too big
   ohki-sugiru kara
bed beddo
bed linen shitsu to
   makurakabah
bedroom shinshitsu/
   beddo ru-mu
bedspread beddo supureddo
beef gyu-niku
beer bihru
before mae ni
beginner shoshinsha
behind ushiro
beige behju
bell beru
below shita
belt beruto
beside soba
best ichiban ih
better motto ih
between aida ni
bicycle jitensha
big ohkih
bikini bikini
bill okanjoh
bird tori
birthday taniyoh bi
   happy birthday!
   otaniyoh bi omedetoh
   birthday present
   taniyoh bi no purezento
biscuit bisketto
bite (verb) kamu (by insect)
   mushi sasare
bitter (adj) nigai
black kuro
blanket mohfu
blind (cannot see) mohmoku
   (no) (on window) buraindo
blister mizu-bukure
blood ketsueki/chi
   blood test ketsueki kensa
blouse burausu
blue ao
boat fune
body karada
boil (verb: water) wakasu
   (noun: on body) hare-mono
boiled yudeta
bolt (on door) boruto
bone hone
bonnet (car) bonn-netto
book (noun) hon
   (verb) yoyaku suru
   bookshop hon ya
booking office kippu uriba
boot (car) toranku
   (footwear) bu-tsu
border kokkyoh
boring tsumaranai

born: I was born in...(place)
   watashi wa... de umare-
   mashita (year) watashi wa...
   nen ni umare-mashita
both ryohhoh
   both of them futari tomo
   both of us watashi tachi
   futari
   both...and... ...to...
bottle bin
bottle opener sennuki
bottom (of box, sea) soko
bowl bohru
box hako
boy otoko no ko
boyfriend bohi-furendo
bra burajah
bracelet udewa/
   buresuretto
braces (trousers)
   zubon-tsuri
brake (noun) burehki
   (verb) burehki o kakeru
branch (office) shiten
brandy burandeh
bread pan
breakdown (car) koshoh
   (nervous) shinkei-suijaku
breakfast chohshoku
breathe iki o suru
   I can't breathe
   iki ga dekimasen
bridge hashi
briefcase kaban
British (things) igirisu no
   the British igirisu jin
brochure panfuretto
broken kowareta
   ...is broken ...ga
   kowarete imasu
   broken leg kossetsu
   shita ashi
brooch burohchi
brother (older) onihsan
   (younger) otohto
brown cha-iro (no)
bruise dabokushoh/
   uchimi
brush (noun) burashi
bucket baketsu
Buddha Hotoke
Buddhism Bukkyoh
Buddhist (noun) Bukkyohto
   (adj) Bukkyoh no
budget (noun) yosan
builder kenchiku ka
building tatemono/biru
bumper banpah
burglar doroboh/yatoh
burn (verb) moyasu
   (noun) yakedo

bus basu
business shigoto; bijinesu
businessman kaisha in
business card meishi
bus station basu teh
busy (person) isogashih
   (crowded) konzatsu shita
but demo
butcher niku ya
butter batah
button botan
buy kau
by: by the window mado no
   soba **by Friday** kinyoh bi
   ma-de ni **by myself** jibun de

C

cabbage kyabetsu
cabinet (kitchen) todana
cable car kehburu kah
cable TV kehbru terebi
café kafe/kissaten
cake kehki
   cake shop kehki ya
calculator kehsanki
call: what's it called?
   nan to ihmasuka
calligraphy shu-ji
camera kamera
can (tin) kanzume **can I
   have...?** ...o onegai shimasu
Canada Kanada
Canadian (person) kanada jin
   (adj) kanada no
cancer gan
candle rohsoku
cap (bottle) futa (hat) bohshi
car kuruma
car park chusha jyo
carburettor kyaburetah
card (business) meishi
cardigan kahdigan
careful chu-i-bukai
   be careful! ki o tsukete
carpenter daiku
carpet jyu-tan/kahpetto
carriage (train) kyakusha
carrot ninjin
carry-cot akachan yoh
   kehtai beddo
car seat (for a baby)
   bebih shihto
case (suitcase) su-tsu-kehsu
cash (money) genkin (coins)
   kohka/koin **to pay cash**
   genkin de harau
cashier (bank, etc.)
   madoguchi
cashpoint "ATM"
cassette kasetto

cassette player *kasetto purehyah*
castle *shiro*
cat *neko*
cave *hora-ana/dohkutsu*
CD drive *CD doraibu*
ceiling *ten-jyoh*
cemetery *bochi*
centre *sentah*
certificate *shohmeisho*
chair *isu*
  swivel chair *kaiten isu*
chambermaid *meido*
change (noun: money) *otsuri*
  (verb, general) *kaeru*
  (verb, transport) *norikaeru*
character (written) *ji*
charger (electrical) *chahjyah*
cheap *yasui*
check-in *chekku in*
check-out (hotel) *chekkuauto*
  (supermarket) *reji*
cheers! *kanpai*
cheese *chihzu*
chemist (shop) *yakkyoku*
cheque *kogitte*
cheque book *kogitte choh*
cherry *sakurambo/cherih*
chess *chesu*
chest *mune*
chewing gum *chu-in-gamu*
chicken *niwatori*
child *kodomo*
children *kodomotachi*
  children's ward
  shohni byohtoh
china *tohki*
China *Chyugoku*
Chinese (person) *chyugoku jin* (adj) *chyugoku no*
chips *poteto-furai*
chocolate *chokorehto*
  box of chocolates
  hakozume no chokorehto
chop (noun: food) *choppu*
  (to cut) *kizamu*
chopstick rest *ohashi-oki*
chopsticks *ohashi*
Christian name *namae*
church *kyohkai*
cigar *hamaki*
cigarette *tabako*
cinema *eiga kan*
city *toshi/machi*
city centre *chu shingai*
class: (train)
  first class *ittoh sha*
  second class *nitoh sha*
classical music
  kurasshikku ongaku
clean (adj) *kireh (na)*

cleaner *seisoh gyohsha*
clear (obvious) *meihaku (na)*
  (water) *sumikitta*
  is that clear?
  wakari-masuka
clever *kashikoi*
client *kokyaku*
clock *tokei* (alarm) *mezamashi-dokei*
close (near) *chikai*
  (stuffy) *iki-gurushih*
  (verb) *shimeru*
  we close at six o'clock
  roku ji ni
clothes *fuku*
club *kurabu* (cards) *kurabu*
coach *choh-kyori basu*
  (of train) *kyakusha*
coach station *basu hacchaku jyo*
coat *kohto*
coathanger *hangah*
cockroach *gokiburi*
coffee *koh-hih*
coins *kohka/koin*
cold (illness) *kaze* (weather) *samui* (food, etc.) *tsumetai*
collar *eri*
collection (stamps, etc.) *shu-shu*
colour *iro*
colour film *karah firumu*
comb (noun) *kushi* (verb) *toku*
come *kuru* **come to my party** *pahtih ni kitene*
  come here! *koko ni kinasai*
  I come from... *...jin desu*
compartment *shikiri kyakushitsu*
complicated *fukuzatsu (na)*
computer *konpyu-tah*
  computer repair shop
  konpyu-tah shu-ri ten
concert *ongakukai/konsahto*
conditioner (hair) *rinsu/ kondishonah*
conductor (orchestra) *shikisha*
conference (meeting) *konferensu* (academic) *gakkai*
congratulations! *omedetoh*
constipation *bempi*
consul *ryohji*
consulate *ryohjikan*
contact lenses *kontakuto renzu*
contraceptive *hinin-yaku* (pills) *hiningu/kondohmu*
contract (noun) *kehyaku sho*
cook (person) *kokku* (verb) *ryohri suru*

cooking utensils *ryohri-dohgu*
cool *suzushih*
cork *koruku*
corkscrew *sen-nuki*
corner *kado*
corridor *rohka*
cosmetics *keshohhin*
cost (verb) *kakaru*
  what does it cost?
  ikura kakari-masuka
cotton *kotton*
cotton wool *dasshimen*
cough (noun) *seki*
country (state) *kuni*
  (not town) *inaka*
cousin *itoko*
cow *ushi*
crab *kani*
cramp *keiren*
crayfish *zarigani*
cream (for face, food) *kurihmu*
credit card *kurejitto kahdo*
crime *hanzai*
crisps *chippu*
crossing (pedestrian) *ohdan hodoh*
crowded *konzatsu shita*
cruise *kohkai/kuru-zu*
crutches *matsubazue*
cry (weep) *naku*
  (shout) *sakebu*
cucumber *kyuri*
cuff links *kafusu botan*
cup *kappu*
cupboard *todana*
curlers *kahrah*
curry *kareh*
curtains *kahten*
customs *zeikan*
cut (noun) *kirikizu* (verb) *kiru*

D

dad *otohsan*
dairy (products) *nyu seihin*
damp *shimetta*
dance *dansu*
dangerous *abunai*
dark *kurai*
daughter *musume san*
  my daughter *musume*
day *hizuke/hi/nichi*
dead *shinda*
deaf *mimi ga tohi*
dear (person) *shitashih*
  (expensive) *takai*
December *jyu-ni gatsu*
deck chair *dekki che-ah*
deep *fukai*

deliberately *wazato*
delivery *haitatsu*
dentist *ha-isha*
dentures *ireba*
deodorant *deodoranto*
department
    (of company, etc.) *bu*
department store *depahto*
departures *shuppatsu*
designer *dezainah*
desk *tsukue/desuku*
develop (a film) *genzoh suru*
diabetic: I'm diabetic
    tohnyoh byoh desu
diamond (jewel) *daiyamondo*
    (cards) *daiya*
diarrhoea *geri*
diary (record of past events)
    nikki (schedule) *techoh*
dictionary *jisho*
die *shinu*
diesel *dihzeru*
different *chigau/betsu (no)*
    I'd like a different one
    betsu no ga hoshih desu
difficult *muzukashih*
dining car *shokudohsha*
dining room *dainingu
    ru-mu; shokudoh*
dinner *yu-shoku/dinah*
directory (telephone)
    denwachoh
dirty *kitanai*
disabled *karada no fujiyu (na)*
dishwasher *shokki araiki*
distributor (in car) *haidenki*
dive *tobikomu*
diving board *tobikomi-dai*
divorced *rikonshita*
do *suru*
doctor *isha*
document *shohsho;
    dokyumento*
dog *inu*
doll *nin-gyoh*
dollar *doru*
door *doa*
double room (hotel)
    daburu ru-mu
    (ryokan) *hutari-beya*
doughnut *dohnatsu*
down *shita*
drawer *hikidashi*
drawing pin *oshi pin*
dress (noun) *doresu*
drink (verb) *nomu*
    (noun) *nomimono*
drinking water
    nomimizu
drive (verb) *untensuru*
driver *untenshu*

driving licence
    unten menkyosho
drops (for eyes) *megusuri*
dry *kawaita*
dry cleaner *dorai
    kurihningu ya*
dummy (for baby) *oshaburi*
during: during... *...no aida ni*
dustbin *gomibako*
duster *dasutah*
duty-free *menzei*

E

each (every) *sorezore*
    200 yen each
    sorezore ni-hyaku yen desu
ear *mimi*
early *hayai*
earphones *iyafon*
earrings *iyaringu*
east *higashi*
easy *yasashih/kantan (na)*
egg *tamago*
eight *hachi*
eighteen *jyu-hachi*
eighty *hachi-jyu*
either: either of them
    dochira demo
    either...or... *...ka...*
elastic (noun) *gomuhimo*
elastic band *wagomu*
elbow *hiji*
electric *denki no*
electrician *denki gishi*
electricity *denki*
electronics *denshi-kohgaku*
electronics store *denkiya*
eleven *jyu-ichi*
else: something else
    nanika hokano mono
    someone else
    dareka hokano hito
    anything else?
    nanika hoka ni
e-mail (ih) *mehru*
    e-mail address
    (ih) *mehru adoresu*
embarrassing *hazukashih*
embassy *taishikan*
embroidery *shishyu*
emerald *emerarudo*
emergency *hijoh*
    emergency ward
    kyu-kyu byohtoh
emperor *tennoh*
empty *kara (no)*
end *owari*
engaged (couple) *konyaku
    shita* (telephone)
    hanashichu

engine (motor) *enjin*
engineering (field of study)
    kohgaku
England *Igirisu*
English *igirisu no*
    (language) *eigo*
Englishman *igirisu jin*
Englishwoman *igirisu jin*
enlargement (of
    photography) *hikinobashi*
enough *jyu-bun*
entertainment *goraku*
entrance *nyu-jyoh guchi/
    iriguchi*
envelope *fu-toh*
epileptic: I'm epileptic
    tenkan mochi desu
escalator *esukarehtah*
especially *tokuni*
estimate (noun) *mitsumori*
Europe *Yohroppa*
evening *yu-gata/yoru*
    good evening *konbanwa*
every (morning, day, etc.)
    mai- (all) *subete no*
everyone *minna*
everything *minna/zenbu*
everywhere *doko demo*
executive (person) *jyu-yaku*
exhibition *tenji kai*
example *rei*
    for example *tatoeba*
excellent *saikoh/subarashih*
excess baggage
    chohka-nimotsu
exchange (verb) *kohkan suru*
    can I exchange this?
    kohkan dekimasuka
exchange rate *rehto*
excursion *ensoku/
    kankoh ryokoh*
excuse me! *shitsurei
    shimasu/sumimasen*
exit *deguchi*
expensive *takai*
explain *setsumei suru*
extension (telephone) *naisen*
    (lengthening) *kakuchoh*
eye *meh*
eyebrow *mayu*

F

face *kao*
faint (unclear) *usui/bonyari
    shita* (verb) *kizetsu suru*
    to feel faint *memai ga suru*
fair (funfair) *yu-enchi*
    it's not fair *fukohhei desu*
false teeth *ireba/gishi*
family *kazoku*

fan (folding fan) *sensu*
   (electric) *senpu-ki*
   (enthusiast) *fan*
fan belt *fan beruto*
far *toh-i* **is it far from here?**
   koko kara toh-i desuka
Far East *Kyokutoh*
fare *unchin; ryohkin*
farm *nohjoh*
farmer *nohfu*
fashion *fasshon*
fast *hayai*
fat (of person) *futotta* (on
   meat, etc.) *abura/shiboh*
father *otohsan*
   my father *chichi*
fax machine *fakkusu*
February *ni gatsu*
feel (touch) *sawaru*
   I feel hot *atsui desu*
   I feel like... *...no yoh na
   ki ga shimasu*
felt-tip pen *feruto pen*
ferry *ferih*
fever *netsu*
fiancé(e) *konyakusha/fianse*
field (agricultural) *nohara*
   what's your field?
   gosenmon wa
fifteen *jyu-go*
fifty *go-jyu*
fig *ichijiku*
figures (sales, etc.)
   gohkeh gaku
filling (tooth) *ha no jyu-ten*
   (sandwich) *nakami*
film (cinema) *eiga*
   (camera) *firumu*
filter *firutah*
finger *yubi*
fire *hi* (blaze) *honoh*
fire extinguisher
   shohkaki
firework *hanabi*
first *saisho* (no)
first aid *ohkyu teate*
first floor *ikkai*
fish *sakana*
fishing *sakana tsuri*
   to go fishing *tsuri ni iku*
fishing rod *tsuri zao*
fishmonger *sakana ya*
five *go*
fizzy *tansan no*
flag *hata; furaggu*
flash (camera) *furasshu*
flat (level) *taira (na)*
   (apartment) *apahto*
flat tyre *panku*
flavour *aji*
flea *nomi*

flight *hikoh(ki)*
   flight number... *...bin*
   flight attendant
   kyakushitsu jyohmu in
flip-flops *zohri*
flippers *hire-ashi*
floor (of room) *yuka*
florist *hana ya*
flour *komugiko*
flower *hana*
flute *furu-to*
fly (verb) *tobu* (insect) *hae*
flyover *rittai kohsa*
fog *kiri*
folk music *minzoku ongaku/
   fohku myu-jikku*
food *tabemono*
food poisoning
   shoku chyudoku
foot (on body) *ashi*
football *sakkah* (ball) *bohru*
for: for... *...no tame ni*
   for me *watashi no tame ni*
   what for? *nan no tame ni*
   for a week *isshu-kan*
foreigner *gaikoku jin*
forest *mori*
fork *fohku*
fortnight *ni-shu-kan*
forty *yon-jyu*
fountain *funsui*
fountain pen *mannen-hitsu*
four *shi/yon*
fourteen *jyu-yon/jyu-shi*
fourth *yombamme*
fracture *kossetsu*
free *jiyu (na)* (no cost)
   muryoh
freezer *reitohko*
Friday *kin-yoh bi*
fridge *reizohko*
fried *ageta*
friend *tomodachi*
friendly *shitashimi no aru/
   furendorih na*
front: in front of...
   ...no mae ni
frost *shimo*
frozen foods *reitoh shokuhin*
fruit *kudamono/furu-tsu*
fruit juice *furu-tsu jyu-su*
fry *ageru*
frying pan *furai pan*
full *ippai*
   I'm full *onaka ga
   ippai desu*
full board *shokuji tsuki*
funny *omoshiroi* (odd) *okashih*
furnished: is it furnished?
   kagu tsuki desuka
furniture *kagu*

G

garage (parking) *shako*
   (petrol) *gassorin sutando*
   (repairs) *shu-ri ya*
garden *niwa*
garlic *ninniku*
gate (airport)
   tohjyoh guchi/gehto
gay (happy) *yohki (na)*
   (homosexual)
   homosekusharu
gear *giya*
gear lever *giya rebah*
geisha (girl) *geisha*
get (fetch) *motte kuru*
   have you got...?
   ...o omochi desuka
   to get the train
   densha ni noru
get back: we get
   back tomorrow
   ashita kaerimasu
   to get something back
   kaeshite morau
get in (to car, etc.) *noru*
   (arrive) *tsuku*
get out (of bus, etc.) *oriru*
get up (rise) *okiru*
gift *omiyage; okurimono*
gin *jin*
girl *onna no ko*
girlfriend *gahrufurendo*
give *ageru*
glad *ureshih*
   I'm glad *ureshih desu*
glass *gurasu*
   (for drinking) *gurasu*
glasses *megane*
gloss prints *kohtaku no
   aru purinto*
gloves *tebukuro*
glue *nori*
go *iku* **where are you
   going?** *doko iku no*
   I'm going to... *...ni ikimasu*
golf *gorufu*
golfer *gorufah*
goggles *suichu megane*
gold *kin*
good *ih* **good!** *yokatta*
   good morning
   ohayo gozaimasu
   good evening *konbanwa*
goodbye (informal) *sayonara;*
   (formal) *sayohnara*
government *seifu*
granddaughter
   mago-musume
grandfather *ojihsan*
   my grandfather *sofu*

grandmother *obahsan*
  my grandmother *sobo*
grandson *mago-musko*
grapes *budoh*
grass *kusa*
Great Britain *lgirisu*
green *midori/gurihn*
greengrocer *yao ya*
grey *hai-iro (no)*
grill *guriru*
grilled *yaita*
grocer (shop)
  shokuryoh hinten
ground floor *ikkai*
guarantee (noun) *hoshoh-sho*
  (verb) *hoshoh suru*
guide book *gaido bukku*
guided tour *gaido*
  tsuki tsuah
guitar *gitah*
gun (rifle) *jyu/raifuru*
  (pistol) *pisutoru*
gutter *amadoi*

H

hair *kami*
haircut (for man) *sanpatsu*
  (for woman) *katto*
hairdresser *biyoh in*
hair dryer *doraiyah*
hair spray *heya supureh*
half *hanbun*
  half an hour *sanjippun*
half board *chohshoku to*
  yu-shoku tsuki
ham *hamu*
hamburger *hanbahgah*
hammer *kanazuchi*
hand *te*
handbag *handobaggu*
hand brake *hando burehki*
handkerchief *hankachi*
handle (door) *handoru*
handsome *hansamu (na)*
hand towel *oshibori*
hangover *futsuka-yoi*
happen: when did
  it happen? *itsu*
  okori mashitaka
happy *shiawase (na)*
harbour *minato*
hard *katai*
  (difficult) *muzukashih*
hard lenses (contact)
  hahdo renzu
harmony *chohwa/hahmonih*
hat *bohshi*
hate: I hate... *watashi wa...*
  ga daikirai desu
have *motsu*

I have... *...wa/ga arimasu/*
  imasu; ...o motte imasu
I don't have...
  ...wa/ga arimasen/imasen;
  ...o motte imasen
  can I have...? *...o kudasai*
  have you got...?
  ...o omochi desuka
I have a headache
  zutsu ga shimasu
hay fever *kafunshoh*
he *kare*
head *atama*
headache *zutsu*
headlights *heddo raito*
head office *honsha*
hear *kiku*
hearing aid *hochohki*
heart *shinzoh*
heart attack *shinzoh mahi*
heating *danboh*
heavy *omoi*
heel *kakato*
hello! *konnichiwa*
  (on the telephone)
  moshi moshi
help (noun) *enjo/tasuke*
  (verb) *taskeru*
  help! *taskete*
hepatitis *kan-en*
her: it's her *kanojo desu*
  it's for her *kanojo no desu*
  give it to her *kanojo ni*
  agete kudasai
  her book(s) *kanojo no hon*
  it's hers *kanojo no*
  (mono) desu
high *takai*
hill *oka*
him: it's him *kare desu*
  it's for him *kare no desu*
  give it to him *kare ni*
  agete kudasai
hire *kariru*
his: his shoe(s) *kare no kutsu*
  it's his *kare no (mono) desu*
history *rekishi*
hitchhike *hicchi-haiku*
HIV positive *eichi ai bui*
  kansensya
hobby *shumi*
holiday *yasumi*
  public holiday *kyu jitsu*
home *ie*
homeopathy *dohshu*
  ryoh hoh
honest *shohjiki (na)*
honey *hachimitsu*
honeymoon *shinkon-ryokoh*
horn (car) *kurakushon*
horrible *osoroshih*

horse *uma*
hospital *byoh-in*
hot *atsui*
hot chocolate *kokoah*
hot water bottle *yutampo*
hotel *hoteru*
hour *jikan*
house *ie*
household products
  katei yo-hin
housewife *sengyo-shufu*
how? *doh*
how much? *ikura desuka*
hundred *hyaku*
hungry: I'm hungry
  onaka ga suite imasu
hurry: I'm in a hurry
  isoide imasu
hurt: will it hurt?
  itai desuka
husband *goshujin*
  my husband *otto*

I

I *watashi*
ice *kohri*
ice cream *aisukurihmu*
ice lolly *aiskyandeh*
if *moshi*
ignition *tenka sohchi*
ill *byohki*
immediately *suguni*
impossible *fukanoh*
in: in Japan *Nihon ni*
  in Japanese *Nihongo de*
  in my room *watashi no*
  heya ni
India *Indo*
Indian (person) *indo jin*
  (adj) *indo no*
indicator *winkah*
indigestion *shohka-furyoh*
infection *kansen*
information *johhoh*
information desk
  madoguchi
inhaler (for asthma, etc.)
  kyu-nyu-ki
injection *chu-sha*
injury *kega*
ink *inku*
inn (traditional Japanese)
  ryokan
insect *mushi*
insect repellent
  mush-sasare yobohyaku
insomnia *fuminshoh*
insurance *hoken*
interesting *omoshiroi*
internet *intahnetto*

internet café *netto kafeh*
interpret *tsu-yaku suru*
invitation *shohtai*
invoice (noun)
　sehkyu-sho
Ireland *Airurando*
Irish *Airurando no*
Irishman *airurando jin*
Irishwoman *airurando jin*
iron (metal) *tetsu*
　(for clothes) *airon*
ironmonger *kanamono ya*
is: he/she/it is...
　kare wa/kanojo wa/
　sore wa... desu
island *shima*
it *sore*
itch (noun) *kayumi*
　it itches *kayui desu*

J

jacket *jyaketto*
jacuzzi *jagujih*
jam *jamu*
January *ichi gatsu*
Japan *Nihon*
Japanese (person) *nihonjin*
　(adj) *nihon no*
　(language) *nihongo*
Japanese-style *wafu*
jazz *jazu*
jealous *shitto-bukai*
jeans *jihnzu*
jellyfish *kurage*
jeweller *hohseki shoh*
job *shigoto*
jog (verb) *jogingu suru*
　to go for a jog *jogingu*
　ni iku
joke *johdan*
journey *ryokoh/tabi*
July *shichi gatsu*
jumper *jampah/sehtah*
June *roku gatsu*
just: it's just arrived
　chohdo tsuki-mashta
　I've just got one left
　hitotsu dake nokotte imasu

K

key *kih; kagi*
keyboard *kihbohdo*
kidney *jinzoh*
kilo *kiro*
kilometre *kiromehtoru*
kimono *kimono*
kiss (noun) *kisu*
kitchen *daidokoro*
knee *hiza*

knife *naifu*
knit *amu*
know: I don't know
　shirimasen
Korea *Kankoku*
　North Korea *Kita Chohsen*
　South Korea
　Daikanminkoku
Korean (person) *kankoku jin*
　(adj) *kankoku no*

L

label *raberu*
lace *rehsu*
lady *fujin/jyoseh*
lake *mizu-umi*
lamb *kohitsuji*
lamp *ranpu; denki stando*
lampshade *denki stando*
　no kasa
land (noun) *tochi*
　(verb) *chakuriku suru*
language *gengo*
laptop (computer)
　(nohto) *pasokon*
large *ohkih*
last (final) *saigo (no)*
　last week *senshu*
　last month *sen getsu*
　at last! *tsui ni*
late: it's getting late
　moh osoi desu
　the train is late
　densha wa okurete imasu
laugh *warai*
launderette *koin-randorih*
laundry (place) *kurihningu ya*
　(dirty clothes) *sentaku-mono*
law (field of study)
　hohritsu/hohgaku
lawyer *bengoshi*
laxative *gezai*
lazy: he is lazy *kare wa*
　namake-mono desu
leaf *ha/happa*
leaflet *chirashi*
learn *narau/manabu*
leather *kawa*
leave (go away) *deru/saru*
　(object) *nokosu*
lecture *kohgi*
lecturer *kohshi*
left (not right) *hidari*
　turn left *hidari ni*
　magatte kudasai
left luggage *tenimotsu*
　azukarisho (locker) *rokkah*
leg *ashi*
leisure *reyjah*
lemon *remon*

lemonade *remonehdo*
length *nagasa*
lens *renzu*
less: less than...
　...yori sukunai
lesson *jugyoh*
letter *tegami*
letterbox *yu-bimbako*
lettuce *retasu*
library *toshokan*
licence *menkyo*
life *seikatsu*
lift (in building) *erebehtah*
　could you give me a
　lift? *nosete kure-masenka*
light (not heavy) *karui*
　(not dark) *akarui*
lighter *raitah*
lighter fuel *raitah no gasu*
light meter *roshutsukei*
like: I like... *...ga suki desu*
　I don't like it
　suki dewa arimasen
　I'd like... *...o onegai*
　shimasu; ...o kudasai
lime (fruit) *raimu*
line (underground, etc.) *sen*
lip salve *rippu-kurihmu*
lipstick *kuchi-beni*
liqueur *rikyu-ru*
list *risuto*
literature (field of study)
　bungaku
litre *rittoru*
litter *gomikuzu*
little (small) *chihsai*
　just a little *hon no sukoshi*
liver *kanzoh*
living room *ima/ribingu*
lobster *ise-ebi*
lollipop *boh tsuki kyandeh*
long *nagai*
　how long does it take?
　dono kurai kakari masuka
lorry *torakku*
lost property *wasure-mono*
lot: a lot *takusan*
　not a lot *ohku arimasen*
loud: in a loud voice
　ohgoe de
lounge *raunji*
love (noun) *ai*
　(verb) *ai suru*
lover *koibito*
low *hikui*
luck *un* good luck!
　guddo rakku/ganbatte
luggage *tenimotsu*
luggage rack
　nimotsu-dana
lunch *chu-shoku*

M

magazine zasshi
mail (verb) yu-soh suru
(noun) yu-bin-butsu
make tsukuru
make-up keshohhin
man otoko; danseh; hito
manager manehjyah
map chizu **a map of Tokyo**
Tohkyoh no chizu
March san gatsu
margarine mahgarin
market ichiba
marmalade mahmarehdo
married: I'm married
kekkon shite imasu
martial arts budoh
mascara masukara
massage massahji
mat (straw) tatami
match (light) macchi
(sport) shiai
material (cloth) kiji
matter: what's the
matter? doh shimashitaka
mattress mattoresu
May go gatsu
may be tabun
me: it's me watashi desu
it's for me watashi no desu
give it to me watashi
ni kudasai
meal shokuji
meat niku
mechanic kikai gishi
medicine (tablets, etc.) kusuri
(field of study) igaku
meeting mihtingu; kaigi
melon meron
memory (computer) memori
men (toilet) dansei yoh
to-ee-reh
menu menyu
message messehji
midday shohgo
middle: in the middle
mannaka ni
midnight mayonaka
milk gyu-nyu; miruku
million hyaku-man
mine: it's mine watashi no
(mono) desu
mineral water
mineraru wohtah
minute fun
mirror kagami
mistake machigai
I made a mistake
machigai-mashita
mobile phone kehtai (denwa)

modem modem
monastery shu-dohin
Monday getsuyoh bi
money okane
monkey saru
month tsuki/...gatsu
monument kinenhi
moon tsuki
moped tansha
more motto
morning asa
good morning
ohayo gozaimasu
in the morning asa ni
mosaic mozaiku
mosquito ka
mother okahsan
my mother haha
motorbike ohtobai
motorboat mohtah-bohto
motorway kohsoku-dohro
Mount Fuji fujisan
mountain yama
mountain climbing tozan
mouse (animal) nezumi
(computer) mausu
moustache kuchi hige
mouth kuchi
move ugoku
don't move! ugokanaide
(house) hikkosu
movie eiga
Mr, Mrs, Ms -san
much: not much sukoshi
much better zutto
ih desu
mug kappu
mum okahsan
museum hakubutsu kan
mushroom kinoko
music ongaku
musical instrument gakki
musician ongakuka
mussels mu-rugai
mustard karashi
my: my key(s) watashi
no kagi
mythology shinwa

N

nail (metal) kugi
(finger) tsume
nail file nehru-fairu
nail polish manikyua
name namae
my name is... watashi no
namae wa... desu
nappies omutsu
disposable nappies
kami omutsu

narrow semai
near: near the door
doa no chikaku
near London
Rondon no chikaku
necessary hitsuyoh
neck kubi
necklace nekkuresu
need (verb) iru **I need...**
watashi wa... ga irimasu
...are needed
...ga hitsuyoh desu
needle hari
negative (photo) nega
neither: neither of them
dochira mo... masen
neither...nor...
mo... mo...masen
nephew oi
never kesshite
new atarashih
news nyu-su
newsagent shinbun ya
newspaper shinbun
New Zealand Nyu-jihrando
New Zealander (person)
nyu-jihrando jin
next tsugi **next week** raishu
next month rai getsu
nice suteki (na)
niece mei
night yoru **two nights** (stay
in hotel) ni haku
nightclub naito-kurabu
nightdress nemaki
nine kyu
nineteen jyu-kyu
ninety kyu-jyu
no (response) ihe
I have no money
okane wa arimasen
no entry shin-nyu kinshi
no problem ihdesuyo
noisy urusai; yakamashih
non-smoking (section)
kin-en seki
noodles men rui
north kita
Northern Ireland
Kita Airurando
nose hana
not: not today
kyoh dewa arimasen
he is not here
kare wa koko ni imasen
not that one
sore dewa arimasen
notepad nohto
notes (money) shiheh
nothing nanimo
novel shohsetsu

November *jyu-ichi gatsu*
now *ima*
nowhere *dokonimo*
number (numeral) *su-ji*
(telephone) *bangoh*
number plate
nambah-purehto
nurse *kangoshi*
nut (fruit) *kurumi*
(for bolt) *natto*

O

occasionally *tama ni*
o'clock: ...*o'clock* ...*ji*
October *jyu gatsu*
octopus *tako*
of ...*no* **the name of the**
street *michi no namae*
off-licence *saka ya*
office *jimusho*
office worker *kaisha in*
often *yoku/tabi tabi*
oil *oiru; sekiyu*
ointment *nankoh*
OK *okkeh*
old (thing) *furui*
(person) *toshi o totta*
olive *orihbu*
omelette *omuretsu*
on *ue* **on the table**
tehburu no ue ni
one (numeral) *ichi*
(+ noun) *hitotsu (no)*
one way *ippoh tsu-koh*
onion *tamanegi*
only ...*dake*
open (adj) *aita* (verb) *akeru*
what time do you open?
nanji ni akimasuka
opening times (museums/
libraries) *kaikan jiman;*
(shops/restaurants)
eigyoh jikan
operating theatre
shujyutsu shitsu
opposite: opposite the
hotel *hoteru no hantai gawa*
or *soretomo/aruiwa*
orange (colour) *orenji-iro (no)*
(fruit) *orenji*
orange juice *orenj jyusu*
orchestra *ohkesutora*
order (noun) *chu-mon; ohdah*
ordinary *futsu-no*
our *watashi tachi no*
it's ours *watashi tachi no*
(*mono*) *desu*
out: he's out *kare wa*
gaishutsu shite imasu
outside *soto*

over (more than) *ijyoh*
(above) *ue*
over there *mukoh*
overtake *oikosu*
oyster *kaki*

P

Pacific Ocean *Taiheiyoh*
package (parcel) *kozutsumi*
packet *pakku*
a packet of... ...*hitohako*
pack of cards
kahdo hitokumi
padlock *nankinjoh*
page *pehji*
pain *itai; itami*
paint (noun) *penki*
painting (hobby)
e o kaku koto
pair *futatsu (no)/ittsui (no)*
a pair of shoes
kutsu issoku
Pakistan *Pakistan*
Pakistani (person) *pakistan*
jin (adj) *pakistan no*
pale (face) *kaoiro ga warui*
(colour) *usui*
pancakes *pankehki*
paper *kami*
(newspaper) *shinbun*
parcel *kozutsumi*
pardon? *e? nan desuka*
parents *ryohshin*
park (noun) *kohen*
(verb) *chu-sha suru*
parking: no parking
chuusha kinshi
parking space *shako*
party (celebration) *pahtih*
(group) *dantai*
(political) *seitoh*
passenger *ryokyaku*
passport *pasupohto*
passport control
(entering) *nyu-koku shinsa*
(leaving) *shukkoku shinsa*
path *komichi*
patient (in hospital)
byoh-nin
pavement *hodoh*
pay *harau*
where can I pay?
doko de harae masuka
payment *shiharai*
peach *momo/pihchi*
peanuts *pihnatsu*
pear *nashi*
pearl *shinju/pahru*
peas *mame*
pedestrian *hokohsha*

peg (clothes)
sentaku-basami
pen *pen*
pencil *enpitsu*
pencil sharpener
enpitsu kezuri
penfriend *penparu*
peninsula *hantoh*
penknife *chihsai naifu*
people *hitobito*
(nation) *kokumin*
pepper (condiment) *koshoh*
(vegetable) *pihman*
peppermints
hakka-dorop/minto
per ...*ni tsuki*
per person *hitori ni tsuki*
perfect *kanzen (na)*
perfume *kohsui*
perhaps *tabun*
perm *pahma*
petrol *gasorin*
petrol station
gassorin sutando
petticoat *pechikohto*
phonecard *tereka;*
terehon cahdo
photocopier *kopihki*
photocopy *kopih*
photograph (noun) *shashin*
(verb) *shashin o toru*
photographer *shashinka*
phrase book *furehzubukku*
physics (field of study)
butsuri
piano *piano*
pickpocket *suri*
I've been pickpocketed
surare mashita
picnic *pikunikku*
piece *hitokire/hitotsu*
pig *buta*
pillow *makura*
pilot *pairotto*
pin *pin*
pine (tree) *matsu*
pineapple *painappuru*
pink *pinku*
pipe (for smoking) *paip*
(for water) *suidohkan*
pizza *piza*
place *basho*
plants *shokubutsu*
plaster (for cut)
bansohkoh
plastic *purasuchikku*
plastic bag *binihru-bukuro*
plate *sara*
platform *purrattohohmu*
play (theatre) *geki/shibai*
pleasant *kimochi no ih*

please (give me)
(o) onegai shimasu
(please do) dohzo
plug (electrical) konsento
(sink) sen
plumber haikankoh
pocket poketto
poison doku
police kehsatsu
police officer kehsatsu kan;
omawarisan
police report tsuh-hoh
police station kehsatsu sho
politics seiji
pond ike
poor mazushih
(bad quality)
shitsu ga warui
pop music poppu
pork butaniku/pohku
port (harbour) minato
porter pohtah (railway
station) akaboh
possible kanoh
post (noun) posuto
(verb) posuto ni ireru
post box posuto
postcard hagaki
poster posutah
postman yu-bin haitatsu nin
post office yu-bin kyoku
potato poteto
poultry toriniku
pound (money) pondo
powder kona/paudah
pram uba-guruma
prawn shiba-ebi
king prawn ise-ebi
pregnant: I'm pregnant
ninshin shite imasu
prescription shohohsen
pretty (beautiful)
kireh (na)
price nedan
priest (Shintoh) kannushi
(Buddhist) obohsan
(Christian) bokushi
printer purintah
private kojin (no)
problem mondai
what's the problem?
doh shimashitaka
**profession: what's your
profession?**
goshokugyoh wa
professor kyohjyu
profits ri-eki
public ohyake
pull hiku
puncture panku
purple murasaki

purse saifu
push osu
pushchair uba-guruma
put oku
pyjamas pajama (traditional
Japanese) yukata

Q

quality shitsu
quay hatoba
question shitsumon
queue (noun) retsu
(verb) narabu
quick hayai
quiet shizuka (na)
quite (fairly) kanari
(fully) sukkari

R

rabbit usagi
radiator rajiehtah
radio rajio
radish daikon
railway tetsudoh
rain ame
raincoat reinkohto
raisins hoshi-budoh/rehzun
rare (uncommon) mezurashih
(steak) re-ah
rat dobu-nezumi
raw nama (no)
razor blades kamisori
no ha
read yomu
reading dokusho
reading lamp
dokusho ranpu
ready yohi ga deki-mashita
ready meals
kakoh shokuhin
rear lights tehru-ranpu
receipt reshihto/ryohshyu-sho
reception uketsuke
record (music) rekohdo
(sporting, etc.) kiroku
record player
rekohdo-purehyah
red aka
refreshments nomimono
registered letter
kakitome yu-bin
relatives (family) shinseki
relax yukkuri suru
religion shu-kyoh
remember oboete iru
I don't remember
oboete imasen
rent (verb) kasu
repairs shu-ri

report (noun) hohkoku sho;
repohto
reservation yoyaku
rest (remainder) sono hoka
(relaxation) yasumu
restaurant resutoran
return (come back) kaeru
(give back) kaesu
return (ticket) ohfuku
rice (uncooked) kome
(cooked) gohan
rice cooker sui-hanki
rich (person) kanemochi (no)
(food) kotteri shita
right (correct) tadashih
that's right sohdesu
(direction) migi
turn right
migi ni magatte kudasai
ring (to call) denwa suru
(wedding, etc.) yubiwa
ripe jukushita
river kawa
road dohro; michi
roasted rohsuto shita
rock (stone) ishi (music) rokku
roll (bread) rohru-pan
roof yane
room heya
(space) basho/supehsu
rope tsuna/rohpu
rose bara
round (circular) marui
it's my round
watashi no ban desu
route (bus, etc.) sen
rowing boat bohto
rubber (eraser) keshigomu
(material) gomu
rubbish (refuse) gomi
(poor quality) garakuta
ruby (stone) rubih
rucksack ryukku sakku
rug (mat) shikimono
(blanket) mohfu
ruins haikyo/iseki
ruler (for drawing) johgi
rum ramu
run (person) hashiru
Russia Roshia
Russian (person) roshia jin
(adj) roshia no

S

sad kanashih
safe anzen (na)
safety pin anzen-pin
sailing boat hansen
saki osake
salad sarada

salami *sarami*
sale (at reduced prices) *sehru*
sales (figures) *uri age*
salmon *sake*
salt *shio*
same: the same dress
  onaji doresu
  the same people
  onaji hito
  same again please
  onajino o moh hitotsu
  onegai shimasu
sand *suna*
sandals *sandaru*
sand dunes *sakyu*
sandwich *sando icchi*
sanitary towels
  seiriyoh napkin
satellite TV *sateraito terebi/*
  ehseh terebi
Saturday *doyoh bi*
sauce *sohsu*
saucepan *nabe*
sauna *sauna*
sausage *sohsehji*
say *yu* **what did you say?**
  nan to iware mashitaka
  How do you say...in
  Japanese? *...wa nihongo de*
  nanto ihmasuka
scarf *sukahfu*
school *gakkoh*
science (field of study)
  kagaku
scissors *hasami*
Scotland *Sukottorando*
Scottish *sukottorando no*
screen (computer, etc.)
  gamen
screen door (ryokan) *fusuma*
screen window
  (ryokan) *shoji*
screw *neji*
screwdriver *neji-mawashi/*
  sukuryu doraibah
scroll *makimono*
sea *umi*
seafood *shifudo*
seat *seki*
seat belt *shihto-beruto*
second (adj) *nibamme (no)*
  (time) *byoh*
secretary *hisho*
see *miru*
  I can't see *miemasen*
  I see (understand) *soh*
  desuka/wakarimashita
self-employed *ji-eigyoh*
sell *uru*
seminar *zemi/seminah*
send *okuru*

separate *betsu (no)*
separated (from husband,
  etc.) *wakareta*
September
  kyu gatsu
serious (situation) *jyu-dai (na)*
  (person) *majime (na)*
serviette *napukin*
set (in theatre) *setto*
seven *shichi/nana*
seventeen *jyu-shichi/*
  jyu-nana
seventy *nana-jyu*
several *ikutsuka (no)*
sew *nuu*
shampoo *shanpu*
shave (noun) *hige-sori*
  (verb) *hige o soru*
shaving foam
  hige-soriyoh sekken
shawl *shohru*
she *kanojo*
sheep *hitsuji*
sheet *shihtsu*
shell *kai/kaigara*
sherry *sherih*
Shinto (adj) *shintoh no*
Shintoism *shintoh*
ship *fune*
shirt *shatsu*
shoelaces *kutsu-himo*
shoe polish *kutsu-zumi*
shoe shop *kutsu ya*
shoes *kutsu*
shop *mise*
shopkeeper *tenshu*
shopping *kaimono/shoppingu*
  to go shopping *kaimono*
  ni iku **shopping trolley**
  shoppingu kahto
short (object) *mijikai*
  (person) (se ga) *hikui*
shorts *hanzubon/shohtsu*
shoulder *kata*
shower (bath) *shawah*
  (rain) *niwaka ame*
shower gel *shawah jeru*
shrimp *ebi*
shrine *jinja*
shutter (window) *amado*
  (camera) *shattah*
  siblings *go kyohdai*
  my siblings *kyohdai*
sick (ill) *byohki* **I feel sick**
  kimochi ga warui desu
side (edge) *hashi*
  I'm on her side *watashi*
  wa kanojo no mikata desu
sidelights *saido-raito*
sights: the sights of...
  ...no kenbutsu

sightseeing *kankoh*
silk *kinu*
silver (colour) *giniro (no)*
  (metal) *gin*
simple *kantan (na)/*
  shinpuru (na)
sing *utau*
single (one) *hitotsu*
  (unmarried) *dokushin*
single room *shinguru ru-mu*
single (ticket) *katamichi*
sink (kitchen) *nagashi*
sister (older) *ane*
  (younger) *imohto*
size (clothes) *saizu*
six *roku*
sixteen *jyu-roku*
sixty *roku-jyu*
skid (verb) *suberu*
skin cleanser
  kurenjingu-kurihm
skirt *sukahto*
sky *sora*
sleep (noun) *suimin*
  (verb) *nemuru*
  to go to sleep *neru*
sleeping bag *nebukuro*
sleeping pill *suimin-yaku*
sleeve *sode*
slippers *surippa*
slow *osoi*
small *chihsai*
smell (noun) *nioi* (verb) *niou*
smile (noun) *hohoemi*
  (verb) *hohoemu*
smoke (noun) *kemuri*
  (verb) *tabako o su*
smoking (section)
  kitsu-en seki
snack *sunakku*
snow *yuki*
so: so good *totemo ih*
  not so much...
  sore hodo... dewa arimasen
soaking solution
  (for contact lenses)
  kontaktoyoh hozoneki
soap *sekken*
socks *kutsushita*
soda water *sohdasui*
sofa *sofa*
soft *yawarakai*
soft lenses *softo-renzu*
soil (earth) *tsuchi*
somebody *dareka*
somehow *nantoka/dohnika*
something *nanika*
sometimes *tokidoki*
somewhere *dokoka*
son *musuko san*
  my son *musuko*

song *uta*
soon *moh sugu*
sorry! *gomennasai*
   I'm sorry *sumimasen*
soup *supu*
south *minami*
South Africa *Minami Afurika*
South African
   (person) *minami afurika jin*
   (adj) *minami afurika no*
souvenir *omiyage*
spade (shovel) *suki*
   (cards) *supehdo*
spanner *spana*
spares *yobi-hin*
spark plug *tenka-puragu*
speak *hanasu*
   do you speak...?
   ...o hanashi-masuka
   I don't speak...
   ...wa hanashimasen
speed *supihdo*
spider *kumo*
spoon *supuun*
sport *supohtsu*
sprain *nenza*
spring (season) *haru*
   (mechanical) *bane*
square (in town) *hiroba*
stadium *stajiamu*
stage (in theatre) *butai*
staircase *kaidan*
stairs *kaidan*
stamps *kitte*
stapler *hochikisu*
star *hoshi* (film) *sutah*
start *shuppatsu/sutahto*
   (verb) *shuppatsu suru*
statement (to police)
   hohkoku sho
station *eki*
statue *dohzoh*
steamed (food) *mushita*
steal *nusumu*
   it's been stolen
   nusumare-mashita
steps *kaidan*
stereo: personal stereo
   uohkman
sticky tape *serotehpu*
stockings *sutokkingu*
stomach *onaka*
stomachache *fukutsu*
stop (verb) *tomaru*
   (bus stop) *basutei*
   stop! *tomare*
storm *arashi*
stove (kitchen) *renji*
straight on *massugu*
strawberry *ichigo/sutoroberih*
stream *ogawa*

street *michi/dohro*
string (cord) *himo/kohdo*
   (guitar, etc.) *gen*
student *gakusei*
stupid *baka*
suburbs *kohgai*
sugar *satoh*
suit (noun) *su-tsu*
   (verb) *au/niau*
   it suits you *anata*
   ni niaimasu
suitcase *su-tsu kehsu*
summer *natsu*
sun *taiyoh*
sunbathe *nikkohyoku*
sunburn *hiyake*
Sunday *nichiyoh bi*
sunglasses *sangurasu*
sunny: it's sunny *hi ga dete*
   imasu/tenki ga ih desu
suntan *hiyake*
suntan lotion *hiyake rohshon*
supermarket *su-pah*
supplement (for fares)
   tsuika ryohkin
suppository *zayaku*
surname *myohji*
sweat (noun) *ase*
   (verb) *ase o kaku*
sweatshirt *torehnah*
sweet (not sour) *amai*
   (candy) *kyandih*
swimming *suiei*
   swimming costume
   mizuigi
   swimming pool
   suimingu pu-ru
   swimming trunks
   suiei-pantsu
switch *suicchi*
syringe *chu-sha ki*
syrup *shiroppu*

T
....
table *tehburu*
tablet *jyohzai*
Taiwan *Taiwan*
take *noru*
   I want to take the train
   densha ni noritai desu
   can I take it with me?
   motte itte mo ih desuka
   we'll take it
   kore ni shimasu
take away *mochi-kaeri*
takeoff *ririku*
talcum powder
   tarukamu-paudah
talk (noun) *hanashi*
   (verb) *hanasu*

tall *takai*
tampon *tanpon*
tangerine *mikan*
tap *jyaguchi*
tapestry *tapesutorih*
tax: including tax *zeikomi*
taxi *takushih*
taxi rank *takushih noriba*
tea (Western) *kohcha*
   (Japanese) *ocha*
teacher *sensei*
teahouse *chamise*
team *chihmu*
tea towel *fukin*
telephone (noun) *denwa*
   (verb) *denwa suru/*
   denwa o kakeru
telephone box
   denwa bokkusu
telephone call
   denwa
telephone number
   denwa bangoh
television *terebi*
temperature *ondo*
   (fever) *netsu*
temple *tera*
ten *jyu*
ten thousand *ichi man*
tennis *tenisu*
tent *tento*
terminal (airport) *tahminaru*
than *yori*
thank (verb) *kansha suru*
   thank you *arigatoh*
   thank you very much
   arigatoh gozaimasu
that: that bus *ano basu*
   what's that?
   a-re wa nan desuka
   I think that...
   ...to omoimasu
theatre *gekijyoh*
their: their room(s)
   karera no heya
   it's theirs *karera no*
   (mono) *desu*
them: it's them *karera desu*
   it's for them *karera no*
   desu **give it to them**
   karera ni agenasai
theme park *tehma pahku*
then *sore kara/soshite*
there (near you) *soko*
   (over there) *asoko*
   there is/are...
   ...ga/wa arimasu/imasu
   there isn't/aren't...
   ...ga/wa arimasen/imasen
   is there...? *...ga/wa*
   arimasuka/imasuka

these: these things
  korera no mono/kore
  these are mine
  korera wa watashi no
  (mono) desu
test (medical) kensa
they karera
thick atsui
thief yatoh
thin usui;
  (person) yaseta
thing (abstract) koto
  (concrete) mono
think omou/kangaeru
  I think so soh omoimasu
  I'll think about it
  kangaete mimasu
third sanbamme
thirsty: I'm thirsty
  nodo ga kawaite imasu
thirteen jyu-san
thirty san-jyu
this: this bus kono basu
  what's this? kore wa
  nan desuka
  this is Mr...
  kochira wa...-san desu
those: those things
  sorera no mono/sore
  those are his sorera
  wa kare no (mono) desu
thousand sen
  ten thousand (ichi) man
three san
throat nodo
throat pastilles nodo gusuri/
  nodo ame
through: through Tokyo
  Tohkyoh keiyu
thunderstorm raiu
Thursday mokuyoh bi
ticket chiketto
tie (noun) nekutai
  (verb) musubu
tights sutokkingu; taitsu
time jikan
  what's the time?
  ima nanji desuka
  to be on time
  yotei dohri
timetable jikoku-hyoh
tin (can) kan
tin opener kankiri
tip (money) chippu
  (end) saki
tired tsukareta
  I feel tired tsukare-mashita
tissues tisshu
to: to England Igirisu e
  to the station eki e
toast tohsuto

tobacco tabako
today kyoh
toe ashi no tsumasaki
tofu shop tofu ya
together issho ni
toilet to-ee-reh
toilet paper toiretto pehpah
tomato tomato
tomato juice tomato jyusu
tomorrow ashita
tongue shita
tonic tonikku
tonight konya
too (also) mo
  (excessive) -sugiru
tooth ha
toothache ha-ita
toothbrush haburashi
toothpaste hamigaki
torch kaichu dentoh
tour tsuah
tourist ryokoh-sha
tourist information centre
  kankoh an-naijyo
towel taoru
tower tawah/toh
town machi
town hall shiyakusho
toy omocha
track suit undoh-gi
tractor torakutah
tradition dentoh
traffic kohtsuu
traffic jam kohtsuu-jyu-tai
traffic lights shingoh
trailer (for car) torehrah
train densha
translate honyaku suru
transmission (for car)
  toransumisshon
travel agent ryokoh
  dairi den
traveller's cheques
  toraberahzu chekku
tray obon/toreh
travelling ryokoh
tree ki
trousers pantsu; zubon
try yatte miru/tamesu
Tuesday kayoh bi
tunnel tonneru
tweezers pinsetto
twelve jyu-ni
twenty ni-jyu
twin room tsuin ru-mu
two ni
type taipu
  what type of...do you
  have? donna taipu no...
  desuka
tyre taiya

U

umbrella kasa
uncle ojisan
under shita
underground chikatetsu
underground station
  chikatetsu no eki
underwear shitagi
university daigaku
until... ...ma-de
unusual mezurashih
up ue (upwards) ue ma-de
urgent kyu (na)/isogi no
  it's urgent kinkyu desu
us: it's us watashi tachi desu
  it's for us watashi tachi
  no desu
  give it to us watashi tachi
  ni kudasai
use (noun) shiyoh (verb)
  tsukau **it's no use** yakuni
  tachimasen/tsukae masen
useful yakuni tatsu/benri na
usual itsumo no
usually itsumo

V

vacancy (room) akibeya
vacuum cleaner sohjiki
vacuum flask mahohbin
valley tani
valve ben
vanilla banira
vanity box (ryokan) kyodai
vase kabin
veal koushi no niku
vegetables yasai
vegetarian bejitarian
vehicle kuruma
very totemo
  very much totemo
vest chokki/besuto
video games bideo gehmu
video tape bideo tehpu
view keshiki/nagame
viewfinder fainda
villa bessoh
village mura
vinegar su
violin baiorin
visa biza
visit (noun) hohmon
  (verb) hohmon suru
visitor hohmonsha
  (tourist) ryokoh sha
vitamin tablet bitaminzai
vodka uokkah
voice koe
voicemail boisu mehru

W

wait *matsu*
waiter *uehtah*
  waiter! *sumimasen*
waiting room *machiai shitsu*
waitress *uehtoresu*
Wales *Uehruzu*
walk (noun: stroll) *sanpo*
  (verb) *sanpo suru/aruku*
  to go for a walk *sanpo
  ni iku*
wall *kabe*
wallet *saifu*
war *sensoh*
ward *byohtoh*
wardrobe *yohfuku-dansu*
warm *atatakai*
was: I was
  watashi wa...deshita
  he was *kare wa...deshita*
  she was *kanojo wa...deshita*
  it was *sore wa...deshita*
washing machine *sentaku ki*
washing powder *senzai*
washing-up liquid *shokki
  yoh senzai*
wasp *suzume-bachi*
watch (wristwatch) *udedokei*
  (verb) *miru*
water *mizu*
waterfall *taki*
wave (noun) *nami*
  (verb) *te o furu*
we *watashi tachi*
weather *tenki*
Web site *Web saito*
wedding *kekkonshiki*
Wednesday *suiyoh bi*
week *shu*
welcome! *yohkoso*
well: I don't feel well
  chohshi ga warui desu
wellingtons *nagagutsu*
Welsh *Uehruzu (no)*
were: we were
  watashi tachi wa...deshita
  you were *anata wa...
  deshita* (sing. informal)
  kimi wa...deshita
  they were
  karera wa...deshita
west *nishi*
  the West *seiyoh*
Westerner *seiyoh jin*
Western-style *yohfuu*
wet *nureta*
what? *nani/nandesuka*
wheel (of vehicle) *sharin*
  (steering) *handoru*
wheelchair *kurumaisu*

when? *itsu*
where? *doko*
which? (of two) *dochira*
  (of more than two) *dore*
whisky *uisukih*
white *shiro*
who? *dare/donata* (formal)
whom: with whom? *dare/
  donata to*
why? *naze/dohshite*
wide *hiroi*
wife *okusan*
  my wife *tsuma*
wind *kaze*
window *mado*
windscreen *furonto garasu*
wine *wain/budohshu*
wine list *wain risuto*
wing *tsubasa/hane*
wing mirror *saido mirah*
winter *fuyu*
with (together with)
  ...to issho ni
  I'll go with you
  a nata to issho ni ikimasu
  (using) *...de*
  with a pen *pen de*
  with sugar *satoh iri*
without *...nashi (de)*
  without sugar
  satoh nashide
witness (person)
  shoh nin
woman *onna; jyoseh*
women (toilet) *fujin to-ee-reh*
wood *mori/zaimoku*
wool *yohmoh*
word *kotoba*
work (noun) *shigoto*
  (verb) *hataraku*
  it doesn't work
  ugokimasen
worktop (kitchen) *chohridai*
worse *motto warui*
worst *saiaku (na)*
wrapping paper
  tsutsumi-gami/hohsohshi
wrist *tekubi*
write *kaku*
writing paper *binsen*
wrong: it is wrong
  machigatte imasu

X, Y

x-ray *rentogen*
year *nen*
yellow *ki iro*
yen *yen*
yes *hai*
yesterday *kinoh*

yet *moh*
  not yet *mada*
yoghurt *yohguruto*
you (sing. formal) *anata*
  (sing. informal) *kimi*
  (plural formal) *anata-gata*
  (plural informal) *kimitachi*
young *wakai*
your: your shoe(s)
  (formal) *anata no kutsu*
  (informal) *kimi no kutsu*
yours: is this yours?
  (formal) *kore wa anata
  no desuka*
  (informal) *kore, kimi no*
youth hostel *yu-su hosuteru*

Z

zen *zen*
zen Buddhism *zenshu*
zen garden *zendera no niwa*
zip *chakku/zippah*
zoo *dohbutsuen*

HIRAGANA/KATAKANA TABLES

Japanese is written in three different script systems: *kanji*, *hiragana*, and *katakana* (see p.14). *Kanji* are Chinese pictograms which need to be learnt individually, but *hiragana* and *katakana* are "syllabaries", with each character representing a separate syllable. The full syllabaries are given here to help you work out the characters in a particular word. With time, you will become more familiar with the most common characters.

Hiragana

あ a	か ka	さ sa	た ta	な na
い i	き ki	し shi	ち chi	に ni
う u	く ku	す su	つ tsu	ぬ nu
え e	け ke	せ se	て te	ね ne
お o	こ ko	そ so	と to	の no

は ha	ま ma	や ya	ら ra	わ wa
ひ hi	み mi		り ri	
ふ fu	む mu	ゆ yu	る ru	
へ he	め me		れ re	
ほ ho	も mo	よ yo	ろ ro	を wo
				ん n

Katakana

ア a	カ ka	サ sa	タ ta	ナ na
イ i	キ ki	シ shi	チ chi	ニ ni
ウ u	ク ku	ス su	ツ tsu	ヌ nu
エ e	ケ ke	セ se	テ te	ネ ne
オ o	コ ko	ソ so	ト to	ノ no

ハ ha	マ ma	ヤ ya	ラ ra	ワ wa
ヒ hi	ミ mi		リ ri	
フ fu	ム mu	ユ yu	ル ru	
ヘ he	メ me		レ re	
ホ ho	モ mo	ヨ yo	ロ ro	ヲ wo
				ン n

There are two signs (" and °) that are used to add additional sounds to the characters in the syllabaries. For example, the character ヒ *hi* can become ピ *pi*, て *te* can become で *de*, and ほ *ho* can become ぽ *po*.

In addition, a long dash (–) is used to lengthen *katakana* syllables. For example, the katakana character テ *te* is lengthened to テー *teh* by adding this dash; テーブル *tehburu* (*table*); and the character ピ *pi* is lengthened to ピー *pih*; コピー *kopih* (*photocopy*).

Acknowledgments

The publisher would like to thank the following for their help in the preparation of this book. In Japan: Hajime Fukase, Keihin Kyuko Bus Co., Ltd, Takao Abe, Seitoku Kinen Kaigakan, Koei drug, Ichinoyu group, East Japan Railway Company (JR), East Japan Marketing & Communications, Inc. (JR Higashi Nihon Kikaku), Kenichi Miyokawa, Naoki Ogawa, Yumiko Nagahari. In the UK: Capel Manor College, Toyota (GB), Magnet Kitchens Kentish Town, Canary Wharf plc, St. Giles College, Yo! Sushi.

Language content for Dorling Kindersley by **g-and-w publishing**
Managed by **Jane Wightwick**

Picture research: **Hugh Schermuly, Hajime Fukase**

Picture credits

Key: *t=top; b=bottom; l=left; r=right; c=centre; A=above; B=below*

p4/5 **DK Images:** *br;* p6/7 **Laura Knox:** *cl;* p14/15 **DK Images:** *Paul Bricknell cAl;* **Ingram Image Library:** *cbl, cAr;* p16/17 **Ingram Image Library:** *ctr;* p18/19 **DK Images:** *David Murray tr;* p24/25 **Takehisa Yano:** *cbl,* **Ingram Image Library:** *tcr;* p28/29 **DK Images:** *John Bulmer tcr; Dave King cr;* **Ingram Image Library:** *bcr;* p30/31 **Alamy RF:** *Comstock Images bcl;* **DK Images:** *cl;* p34/35 **Takehisa Yano:** *tcr;* p36/37 **DK Images:** *cbr;* p38/39 **Takehisa Yano:** *bl-r, tcr, cr;* p40/41 **Takehisa Yano:** *bl, tcr, cAr, cr, cBr, cbA, bcr bcrA;* p42/43 **Takehisa Yano:** *bl-r, c, cr, crB;* p44/45 Courtesy of **Toyota (GB):** *c;* p46/47 **Toyota (GB):** *ctr;* **Ingram Image Library:** *cAr;* **Takehisa Yano:** *cr, cl, cAl;* p48/49 **Takehisa Yano:** *c, bl, cr;* p50/51 **Takehisa Yano:** *tcr;* **Alamy:** *Peter Titmuss cr;* p52/53 **Getty:** *Stone: Kiriko Shirobayashi cl,* **Alamy RF:** *Image Farm Inc cAr;* **Takehisa Yano:** *bl-r, cr, cBr;* p54/55 **Alamy:** *Frank Herholdt bcl; Jackson Smith cBl;* **Alamy RF:** *BananaStock cl; John Foxx c;* **ThinkStock** *tcr;* **DK Images:** *Andy Crawford bclA;* p56/57 **Takehisa Yano:** *cl, cAl;* **Toyota (GB):** *bl, cBr;* p58/59 **Alamy RF:** *Brand X Pictures cBl; Image Source cAAl;* **DK Images:** *John Heseltine cr;* p60/61 **Alamy RF:** *Image Source cAr;* **DK Images:** *Steve Gorton cAAr; Pia Tryde cAr;* p62/63 **DK Images:** *Russell Sadur cBr, Jo Foord cr;* **Takehisa Yano:** *bl-r, c;* **Alamy RF:** *Goodshoot cAr;* p64/65 **Alamy:** *Arcaid bcrA;* **Alamy RF:** *Diana Ninov cAr;* **Ingram Image Library:** *tcr;* p66/67 **Alamy:** *Arcaid cll;* **Ingram Image Library:** *bcr;* **Alamy RF:** *Image Source cr;* **Takehisa Yano:** *bl;* p68/69 **Takehisa Yano:** *clAl, clAr, cll, clBl, clBr, ctr, cAr cBr, cbr;* p72/73 **Alamy RF:** *Image Source cAr; Comstock Images tcr;* p74/75 **Alamy RF:** *Doug Norman bl;* p76/77 **Takehisa Yano:** *bcl, bcll, bclll, bcAl, bcAll, cbr;* p80/81 **Getty:** *Taxi / Rob Melnychuk bc;* **Ingram Image Library:** *cAr;* **Xerox UK Ltd:** *tcr;* p82/83 **Alamy:** *wildphotos.com tcr;* **Alamy RF:** *Momentum Creative Group cAl;* **Ingram Image Library:** *cl;* p84/85 **Alamy:** *Brand X Pictures cr;* **Alamy RF:** *SuperStock tr;* **Ingram Image Library:** *crB;* p86/87 **Getty:** *Taxi / Rob Melnychuk tc;* p90/91 **DK Images:** *cl; David Jordan cAr; Stephen Oliver cr;* **Ingram Image Library:** *cBr;* p92/93 **Ingram Image Library:** *cl;* **Alamy RF:** *Pixland cr;* **DK Images:** *Guy Ryecart tr;* p94/95 **Alamy RF:** *ImageState Royalty Free bcr;* **DK Images:** *tcr;* p96/97 **DK Images:** *ctl;* p98/99 **Getty Images:** *Daisuke Morita c;* **Alamy:** *Ian Lambot bl;* p102/103 **Garden Picture Library:** *Marie O'Hara b;* **DK Images:** *tcr; James Young cAAr;* p104/105 **DK Images:** *Bob Langrish cl(6); Jane Burton bcl; Geoff Dann cl(2); Max Gibbs cl(4); Frank Greenaway cl(3); Tracy Morgan c(5);* p106/107 **Getty Images:** *Daisuke Morita cr;* p110/111 **Alamy RF:** *Stockbyte cl;* p112/113 **Ingram Image Library:** *bl;* p116/117 **Takehisa Yano:** *bcl, bc, bcr;* p118/119 **Alamy RF:** *Pixland tcr;* **Corbis:** *Michael S. Yamashita c;* p120/121 **Alamy:** *ImageState / Pictor International cl;* **DK Images:** *bcl;* p122/123 **DK Images:** *Judith Miller / Sparkle Moore at The Girl Can't Help It cl;* p124/125 **DK Images:** *Bob Langrish cl(6); Jane Burton bcl; Geoff Dann cl(2); Max Gibbs cl(4); Frank Greenaway cl(3); Tracy Morgan c(5);* **DK Images:** *Clive Streeter tl;* **Alamy:** *ImageState / Pictor International cl;* **DK Images:** *bcl;* p126/127 **Takehisa Yano:** *cl, cll, clll;* **Alamy RF:** *Image Farm Inc bl;* p128 **DK Images:** *Clive Streeter tl.*

All other studio and location images: **Mike Good**